ARIZONA
HIGHWAYS
WILDLIFE GUIDE

125 of Arizona's Native Species

By Brooke Bessesen

Text: Brooke Bessesen
Editor: Kelly Vaughn
Copy Editor: Noah Austin
Photographs: The Arizona Game and Fish Department and *Arizona Highways* Contributors
Designer: Keith Whitney
Photo Editor: Jeff Kida

With special assistance from the Arizona Game and Fish Department

Library of Congress Control Number: 2015959730
ISBN: 978-0-9971247-0-5
First printing, 2016. Printed in China.

Published by the Book Division of *Arizona Highways* magazine, a monthly publication of the Arizona Department of Transportation, 2039 W. Lewis Avenue, Phoenix, Arizona, 85009.
Telephone: 602-712-2200
Website: www.arizonahighways.com

Publisher: Win Holden
Associate Publisher/Marketing Director: Kelly Mero
Editor: Robert Stieve
Managing Editor/Books: Kelly Vaughn
Associate Editor: Noah Austin
Creative Director: Barbara Glynn Denney
Art Director: Keith Whitney
Photography Editor: Jeff Kida
Production Director: Michael Bianchi
Production Coordinator: Annette Phares

Front Cover: Coyote, by Yvonne Kippenberg

White-nosed coati, pg. 41

Contents

Coues white-tailed deer (male)

For Dad, who would have loved this book best of all.

My heartfelt thanks to everyone who helped shape this guide — the expert photographers, biologists, editors, designer, production team and reviewers. We share this accomplishment as one.

— Brooke Bessesen

Preface

I officially started writing about animals at age 7, when I penned an enthusiastic report on birds. It began: *birds can fly! birds liv in nests! birds eat birdseed or wirms! some birds chirp and some don't! if you play with baby birds the dad will poke you with his bill!* My thesis, informed by backyard observations and a weighty set of *Encyclopaedia Britannica*, ran a riveting 15 pages and — in all likelihood — set me on course to write this book. Between those sentences and these, my passion for wildlife has never wavered. After decades of study, it is a privilege to lead this tour into the world of Arizona wildlife.

What makes this guidebook special is that it covers many types of animals — mammals, birds, reptiles and amphibians. Even a few fish. Its pages are plump with details to describe Arizona's most iconic, concerning, intriguing and unexpected species. And, of course, the most common ones, too. So if you spot an animal from your kitchen window or your car, or while hiking up a trail, you'll probably find it somewhere in here. While this book does not include every possible species, it is a hearty introduction to native wildlife and should satisfy your curiosity.

Of course, reading is only half the journey. Once you've perused its pages, please pocket this guide and get outdoors to where the animals transform from still photos and typeset words into strolling, sniffing, flapping, breathing individuals. Perhaps you'll spy a beaver plucking summer grass to soften its nest. Or spot a bighorn leaping from ledge to ledge on a ruddy butte. Or laugh at the antics of a playful raven or a clever heron luring fish closer with a morsel of picnic bread. Whatever the experiences, they will be yours to keep. My personal hope is that some youngster, fascinated by nature, will use this book to better understand his or her outdoor discoveries and write a report. Who can say where that might lead?

Using This Guidebook

Animal chapters

The animals selected for this guidebook are but a sampling of the total that call Arizona home, so this book is a condensed yet broad introduction to wildlife within the state. The four chapters cover the five traditional classes of vertebrates (animals with a spine).

Mammals (class *Mammalia*) have some amount of hair, and females give live birth and produce milk to nourish their offspring. They also are endothermic, meaning they can produce their own internal heat and stay active in cold weather. Humans are mammals, which is why we may feel a strong connection to other species within this class (who doesn't love wolves, lions and rabbits?). Unfortunately for wannabe observers, most mammals are nocturnal (see viewing tips on page 150).

Birds (class *Aves*) are direct descendants of theropod dinosaurs. Like mammals, they are endothermic, but they lay eggs and have feathers and wings, and most possess lightweight, honeycombed bones for flight. Because the majority of avian species are diurnal (like us) and often have brightly colored plumage — and several rank extremely high on the intelligence scale — these animals attract a lot of human attention. A raptor ID chart is on page 68.

Reptiles (class *Reptilia*) are egg-layers that have scales instead of feathers or fur. Turtles, snakes and lizards make up this group. Being ectothermic, they cannot regulate their own body temperature and so rely on their surroundings for heating and cooling. Some reptiles are diurnal, while others are nocturnal. During winter in Arizona, most disappear to brumate, a kind of reptilian hibernation.

Amphibians (class *Amphibia*) and fish (class *Osteichthyes*) share a chapter. Amphibians are ectothermic (like reptiles), but because their skin lacks protective scales, they must stay moist, so amphibians live near or in water. Frogs, toads and salamanders are amphibians. These egg-laying animals always begin their lives in water as aquatic larvae, but most metamorphose into air-breathing adults that can also travel by land. Most are crepuscular or nocturnal in their activities.

Fish lay eggs and are fully aquatic throughout their lives, possessing gills to extract oxygen from the water and fins for swimming. These ectothermic animals are often crepuscular, found year-round in many lakes, ponds and waterways throughout Arizona.

Arizona's official state animals

 Did you know Arizona has six state animals? Perhaps you have heard of the state mammal (ringtail) or state bird (cactus wren). But there also are a state reptile (ridge-nosed rattlesnake), state amphibian (Arizona treefrog) and state fish (Apache trout). (Even an invertebrate was designated — a state butterfly, the two-tailed swallowtail.) Each chapter highlights these species, marked with the icon shown above.

Finding an animal

The animals in this book are sorted by relatedness. To find a particular animal, you may browse the section with similar animals or use the index at the back of the book to locate an

Cooper's hawk

COOPER'S HAWK
Accipiter cooperii

DESCRIPTION: Slate gray above and barred rufous below; dark cap and reddish eyes; long tail with dark bands and rounded trailing edge
SIZE: Length of 14 to 18 inches; wingspan of 2 to 3 feet; weight of up to 1 pound; female larger than male
DIET: Mostly birds; some small mammals and lizards
HABITAT: Woodlands, forests and urban areas
DISTRIBUTION: Statewide; migrates away from the hottest southwestern deserts during summer
NEST AND EGGS: Cupped stick pile, usually in a tree; three to five eggs, incubation 34 to 36 days
● This crow-sized bird has short, rounded wings and a long, narrow tail for excellent aerial maneuverability — it flies with a quick rhythm of "flap, flap, flap ... glide." Hatching Cooper's hawks have gray-green eyes, which turn bright yellow in juveniles before transitioning to the deep red of adulthood. The male does most of the hunting for his family through the nesting period (four to five weeks).
SIMILAR SPECIES: The sharp-shinned hawk (similar range) has near-identical plumage but is smaller (about 12 inches) with a slightly shorter, squared-off tail.

AMERICAN KESTREL
Falco sparverius

DESCRIPTION: Rusty red back, gray-blue wings, cinnamon tail with black bar near tip; female is ruddy brown above, pale-streaked underparts and several dark, muted bars on tail; both sexes have gray crown and two dark, vertical cheek stripes
SIZE: America's smallest falcon, with length of 8.5 to 12 inches; wingspan of up to 2 feet; weight of 3 to 6 ounces; female larger than male
DIET: Mostly invertebrates (especially

American kestrel

grasshoppers); some birds, lizards and rodents
HABITAT: Desert scrub, grasslands, woodlands, forests, agricultural land and urban areas
DISTRIBUTION: Statewide
NEST AND EGGS: Cavity (woodpecker hole or nest box); four or five eggs, incubation 29 to 31 days
● This is one of only a few raptors that show sexual dimorphism in coloring as well as size. Bird counts suggest kestrels are declining in Arizona, yet they are still widespread and fairly prevalent — often seen perched upon fence posts and telephone wires, bobbing their tails. Their call is a rapid killy-killy-killy! In flight, wings are distinctly pointed, and these agile predators have the ability to hover, briefly holding position before diving down to seize prey. They have been reported to cache food, sometimes out in the open.

AMERICAN PEREGRINE FALCON
Falco peregrinus anatum

DESCRIPTION: Dark gray above, buffy underparts with barred belly and thighs; black helmet extends down in sideburns; long, pointed wings appear swept back in flight
SIZE: Length of 14 to 19 inches; wingspan of about 3.5 feet; female larger than male
DIET: Primarily birds (caught in flight); some bats; occasionally steals from other raptors
HABITAT: Desert scrub, grasslands, canyons, wetlands and urban areas; especially near cliffs
DISTRIBUTION: Statewide; year-round in moderate elevations, summer in highest mountains and winter in lowest deserts
NEST AND EGGS: Scraped depression on high cliff, bridge or building ledge; three or four eggs, incubation 33 to 35 days
CONSERVATION STATUS: Removed from endangered-species list in 1999
● Here is the world's fastest animal! A peregrine can fly level at nearly 70 mph and — wings tucked for a dive — has been clocked at speeds over 230 mph! With such aerobatic prowess, it is a proficient hunter. Peregrine means "wandering," and many do seasonally migrate around the state. Mating pairs appear monogamous. The male may help incubate eggs, and both parents deliver food to their nestlings, which fledge in about one and a half months. The peregrine falcon once was endangered. In the mid-20th century, its eggs suffered thinning effects from the insecticide DDT, causing populations to fall into rapid decline. As with bald eagles, the species took decades to recover.

American peregrine falcon

LAURN RICHEY
TOP: PEGGY COLEMAN; ABOVE: A. O. TUCKER

---

exact page number for the species you seek. A few special groups (bats, squirrels, woodpeckers, hummingbirds, ducks, rattlesnakes, toads and fish) are presented together, each with an introduction to familiarize you with common characteristics.

Understanding the information fields

For each entry, you will find the species' common name and *Scientific name*, followed by some intriguing natural-history notes and interesting tidbits about its ecology and life, and quick details to help you identify the species. Occasional *Living With Wildlife* sidebars offer tips or address common concerns that will help keep encounters safe and rewarding for both you and the animals.

Description

A brief description gives you simple identifiers for the species. These are based on the most common or recognizable appearance of an adult. If sexually dimorphic, the male is described first, followed by notes for the female. Seasonal variances, especially in avian plumage, may or may not be mentioned. Juveniles, often unlike adults, are not described for most animals.

Size

Size (or length) is based on an average adult. When listed separately, head and body plus tail equals total length. When height is listed, it is to the top of the head, not the shoulders.

Diet

Diet focuses on common foods and may not include everything that species has been reported to eat.

Habitat

Here you will find the type(s) of terrain in which the species is known to exist. While at least 14 specialized ecosystems have been identified in Arizona, a measure of simplification has been applied in this book. Broad-scope environments include desert scrub, grasslands, woodlands, forests and riparian areas. For some animals, the habitat may be a bit more detailed (e.g.

canyons or cienegas) or explicit locations might be suggested, such as "under rocks," "areas with heavy vegetation" or "slow-moving streams." In some cases, elevation is listed, too.

Distribution

This is the general range within the state of Arizona. It gives an idea where the animal may be found, although a species might utilize only certain habitats within that given range.

Conservation status

 Some species are protected under the Endangered Species Act (ESA) and are listed as either endangered (at serious risk of extinction or extirpation) or threatened (likely to become endangered). All conservation species have strict management protocols. Since those animals may be especially exciting to see, an Arizona Conservation Species icon helps you readily identify them. It's important to note that most

native species, while not designated under the ESA, still are legally protected in Arizona.

Similar species

Brief notes about similar species may assist you in identifying closely related or look-alike animals. Be sure to read these — especially if you find an animal that seems sort of like the one presented, but looks a little different and/or is outside the cited distribution range. Most of the similar species do not have their own entry in this book.

Nest and eggs (birds only)

A brief description of the nest is followed by information about the eggs, including the typical number and reported incubation period.

Venom (certain snakes)

For animals marked VENOMOUS at the top of their entries, venom potency and yield are provided, along with any interesting or related notes.

Call (frogs only)

For each species, you will find a description and length of call.

Wildlife viewing areas

After the animal entries comes a chapter with ideas for how and where to (hopefully) spot some Arizona species. It includes five highly recommended sites from around the state — one per region — providing a range of both landscapes and land-preservation systems: national park, state park, wildlife area, national wildlife refuge and national monument. The map on page 143 shows their general locations.

Each viewing area has a written description, followed by information fields for the year it was established, size of the area, elevation, the types of habitat within its boundaries and, of course, some of the wildlife that might be sighted there. To assist you in planning a trip, there are also basic directions, a note on whether there is an entry fee or trails to access, plus a list of services and facilities to guide you with packing and preparation. The phone number and website address ensure you can get more information if needed.

Black-footed ferrets are protected under the Endangered Species Act.

A Primer on Taxonomy

Knowing the basics of taxonomy will help you visualize and appreciate the connectedness of all animals. While the subject might appear a bit scholarly at first with so many Latin- or Greek-derived words, it's really not difficult to grasp. Stick with it, and soon you will have an insider's view of the colossal family tree — the tree of life — on which our own leaves flutter.

Taxonomy is a classification system that divides living organisms into groups, called taxons. It has a fairly simple structure where every level divides into more closely related organisms. To begin, all animals belong to kingdom *Animalia*. Below that, all furry, feathered or scaled animals are gathered in phylum *Chordata*, subphylum *Vertebrata* (vertebrates, animals with a spine). Next come the more recognized levels: class, order, family, genus and then species. Genus and species make up an animal's scientific name — they are always together and always italicized. Take the commonly named rock squirrel. It is in class *Mammalia* (mammals), order *Rodentia* (rodents), family *Sciuridae* (squirrels), then genus *Otospermophilus* (ground squirrels), and the species is *variegatus* (Latin for variegated, because its fur is delicately mottled). So the rock squirrel's scientific name is *Otospermophilus variegatus*, which, once stated, can be shorted to *O. variegatus*.

Occasionally, there is a further division to subspecies, and that name is tagged onto the end. An example is the Sonoran pronghorn, a subspecies of the American pronghorn and, thus, scientifically named *Antilocapra americana sonoriensis*.

All that said, an animal's placement is not set in stone, because taxonomy is slowly, yet perpetually, redefined by the latest discoveries. The most current precepts are used in this book, but change is on the horizon. Traditionally, taxons have been rooted in common characteristics — how animals look and, in some cases, how they act. Now, genetic tests are revising the system, creating DNA-based taxons called clades. And modern studies have exposed some unexpected evolutionary relationships. For example, a 2008 *Science* article revealed that, genetically speaking, falcons are more closely related to parrots than they are to hawks. Talk about shaking the family tree. Remember, science is driven by questions. Ask, ask, ask, and bit by bit, possible answers emerge, titillating buds of information that make animal ancestry a compelling subject.

MAMMALS

Hoofed	(*Artiodactyla*)
Bats	(*Chiroptera*)
Opossums	(*Didelphimorphia*)
Carnivores	(*Carnivora*)
Rodents	(*Rodentia*)
Rabbits, Hares	(*Lagomorpha*)

BIRDS

Daytime Raptors	(*Falconiformes*)
Owls	(*Strigiformes*)
Woodpeckers	(*Piciformes*)
Nighthawks	(*Caprimulgiformes*)
Doves	(*Columbiformes*)
Turkeys, Quail	(*Galliformes*)
Hummingbirds	(*Apodiformes*)
Perching Birds	(*Passeriformes*)
Roadrunners	(*Cuculiformes*)
Ducks	(*Anseriformes*)
Herons	(*Pelecaniformes*)
Coots	(*Gruiformes*)
Grebes	(*Podicipediformes*)
Killdeer	(*Charadriiformes*)

REPTILES

Turtles	(*Testudines*)
Lizards, Snakes	(*Squamata*)

AMPHIBIANS & FISH

Frogs	(*Anura*)
Salamanders	(*Caudata*)
Bony Fishes	(class *Ostheichthyes*)

Arizona's Habitats

A variety of elevations

Arizona is known for its varied terrain, a shifting landscape of cactus and stone. Angular mountains give way to vast pastel valleys, and rivers draw languid zigzags where droopy willows and cottonwoods meet to drink. Indeed, one of the great gifts of residence is that you can drive in any direction and enjoy a change of scenery. The American Southwest is, by and large, considered desert, marked by a harsh, arid clime. Yet Arizona is full of topographical surprises. Throughout the state's 114,000 square miles, the earth rises and falls in fantastic landforms: plateaus, canyons, pinnacles and dunes. And with elevations spanning from near sea level along the Colorado River to more than 12,600 feet atop Flagstaff's San Francisco Peaks, there are dramatic transitions from desert scrub to grasslands to cooler woodlands and forests; there is even a stipple of alpine tundra at the tip of Humphreys Peak. These diverse environments, punctuated by rare and extraordinary wetlands, allow inhabitation by a wide range of plants and animals. In fact, Arizona ranks third in the United States for overall biodiversity.

What makes a desert a desert?

A desert is described as an extremely arid geographical zone, featuring clear skies and sparse vegetation. There are four separate deserts in the American Southwest, and Arizona is the only state that contains portions of all of them. Although each one is distinct in temperature, flora and fauna, craggy rocks and prickly plants prevail, whether you are exploring the northerly Great Basin Desert, with elevations as high as 7,200 feet and the potential for snow; the northwestern, wind-blown Mohave Desert, home of the peculiar Joshua tree; the vast stretches of the southeastern Chihuahuan Desert, the largest in North America; or the southwestern, saguaro-strewn Sonoran Desert, the hottest, yet most bio-rich, of the four.

Grasslands and woodlands and forests, oh my!

In such a checkerboard of landscapes, habitats may intermingle. At least 14 specialized ecosystems have been recognized within the state, but, for simplicity's sake, this book adheres to those most familiar. Grasslands, flat or rolling stretches of open and grass-covered terrain, may be found at elevations as low as 3,600 feet and as high as 11,480 feet. Woodlands, mottled with oak, piñon and/or juniper trees, occur between 4,250 and 7,500 feet. Forests of pine, fir and/or spruce trees grow higher, up at 6,500 to 12,500 feet, and receive the most rainfall per year, at 18 to 39 inches.

Truly precious wetlands

With only 0.3 percent of its land area covered by water, Arizona is the second-driest state in the nation (behind New Mexico). That makes water an incredibly valuable resource not just for humans, but for wildlife, too. The state has two rainy seasons, winter and summer, and they provide the bulk of moisture for the entire year. The summer rainy season, a complex weather phenomenon called the Southwestern monsoon, produces thunderstorms from July to September. It may deliver up to 70 percent of the southern desert region's annual rainfall and plays a critical role in the breeding ecology of many native species. Much of that rainfall is absorbed into parched soil to nourish thirty plants. Only a portion reaches natural water stores — rivers, lakes, marshes and ponds —

and those limited supplies must sustain everyone through the dry season. It is essential to understand that wetlands are the lifeblood of the desert, serving as habitat for hundreds of species (especially birds) that otherwise would not be able to survive in the arid clime.

The Madrean Archipelago – Arizona's "sky islands"

Among all of Arizona's bountiful habitats, perhaps the most unique exists in its southeastern reaches. In a 1943 issue of *Arizona Highways* magazine, Natt Dodge described the Chiricahua Mountains as "a mountain island in a desert sea." The term "sky island" later was coined to describe any mountain (or range) with species that, specialized to their montane habitat, never cross the surrounding lowlands. In such geographic isolation, endemic species arise and are found nowhere else on Earth. There are 40 sky islands clustered at the convergence of the massive Rocky Mountains and the Sierra Madre Occidental, and they're collectively referred to as the Madrean Archipelago. These extraordinary

mountains harbor dozens of rare and endemic species. As you can imagine, sky-island species, with such limited distribution, are at particular risk for extinction. An example is the endangered green-and-red thick-billed parrot, which used to reside in Arizona's sky-island forests but now is extirpated from the state.

The acclaimed Grand Canyon

Arizona is known as the Grand Canyon State. The namesake chasm, carved into ancient stone by the mighty Colorado River, marks the northeastern region of the state. As one of the Seven Natural Wonders of the World, it hosts a spectacular array of wildlife. Shifting temperatures caused by the Canyon's 1-mile elevation drop — potentially more than a 25-degree increase from rim to river — divide the landscape into layers, each a habitat dominated by particular flora and fauna. With normally distant species thriving in vertical proximity, overall biodiversity is truly remarkable. There are even endemics, like the Grand Canyon pink rattlesnake and the charming Kaibab squirrel.

Gila monster

Arizona's Wildlife

So many species

Owing to its miscellany of habitats, Arizona is home to more than 1,500 recorded animal species, nationally ranking fifth for diversity of mammals, third for birds and second for reptiles. The state's 28 species of chiropterans earn it second place for bats. And it tops the charts with 13 species of rattlesnakes. In fact, the Grand Canyon State takes an unexpected eighth place in overall vertebrate diversity. Enormous or tiny, feathered or furred, moist or scaly, Arizona's native wildlife runs the gamut in shape and dimension. Some species are exquisite to behold, while others are appreciated for having special character. There are predators and prey, tool-users, singers and travelers. Yes, a few venomous species, too. But never fear — every animal has its own special place in the system.

Adapted to desert living

In order to survive natural changes on Earth — gradual, creeping shifts in habitat — animals must adapt. These adaptations — physical or behavioral traits that evolve slowly, over thousands (or millions) of years — allow species to thrive in particular ecosystems. Desert dwellers require many adaptations. For example, in the hot, dry, often-barren habitat of Arizona, inhabitants tend to be smaller than their northern counterparts — better to shed heat. Many are nocturnal, taking daytime respite in burrows, caves and crevices. Others migrate to higher elevations in the summer. Although most animals visit water sources to drink, some, especially small and less-mobile ones, drink little or no water, absorbing moisture only from their food. Camouflage is another important desert adaptation — without a lot of foliage to conceal predators from prey, and vice versa, native species are likely to be tan or brown so they can blend in with rocks and sand. Even breeding seasons may shift in the desert, either because spring-like weather comes earlier in the year or to coincide with periods of abundance provided by the rainy season(s). It's interesting to consider how and why species become adapted to life in the extremes.

Wildlife and us

Humans have inhabited Arizona for more than 12,000 years, but in the Anthropocene epoch of the past two centuries, we have put increasing pressure on the environment and animals that depend on it. Urbanization, clear-cutting for agriculture, cattle-grazing, pollution and water diversions (which alter and fragment riparian corridors) all negatively affect wildlife. Add in wildfires, invasions of non-native species and a drought-inducing warming trend, and it's no surprise that some species are struggling to survive. If we build and consume without caution, wildlife is sure to be lost. And if keystone species, animals that play an imperative role in the functioning of the ecosystem, begin disappearing (some are already endangered), the whole desert environment could destabilize. Don't feel daunted; we simply have to ask ourselves a couple of questions: *How does wildlife enrich and benefit our lives? How can we help those animals thrive?* Living in cities, surrounded by buildings and cars, we may not feel as connected with nature as we'd like to be. Still, every resident can play a role in desert conservation, especially by limiting water use. I am confident you will find the effort imperative once you've traveled and experienced the natural splendor of Arizona.

Bobcat

MAMMALS

ELK
Cervus elaphus

DESCRIPTION: Muscular frame; dark brown overall (grayer in winter, redder in summer), whitish rump; thick neck, shaggy on buck; male antlers branch into multiple tines and span up to 5 feet
SIZE: Length of 6 to 9 feet, plus tail of 4 to 7 inches; height of up to 9 feet (including antlers); typical weight of 450 to 800 pounds (males occasionally reach 1,100 pounds); male larger than female
DIET: Mostly grasses; some forbs and woody plants
HABITAT: Forests, woodlands and montane meadows; from 7,000 to 10,500 feet in summer, down to 5,500 feet in winter; usually within half-mile of water
DISTRIBUTION: From Grand Canyon's South Rim to White Mountains along Mogollon Rim
■ Elk are in the deer family (*Cervidae*). All male deer grow antlers, which bud from plates on the skull, called pedicles, and quickly extend, covered with velvety skin that supplies blood to the developing bone. Once the antlers are full length, the skin dies and peels away, exposing hardened spikes used during rut to battle other males and attract females. After mating season, the antlers loosen at the pedicles and fall off. Elk bulls are renowned for crepuscular bugling, rising squeals that echo through the autumn forest. Harems averaging 15 to 20 cows begin forming by September. As with other mammals, the male mounts the female during mating. In early summer, following an eight-month pregnancy, an elk mother drives away her yearling and finds a secluded spot to deliver a new calf, which is left alone — tucked and motionless — for lengthy periods between nursing. Baby elk (mule deer and white-tailed deer, too) are reddish-brown with white spots that provide camouflage in the dappled woods. This species can maintain a traveling speed up to 30 mph, is capable of vertical jumps of 8 to 10 feet and is a proficient swimmer. Arizona's native subspecies, Merriam's elk (*C. e. merriami*), was pushed into extinction. In 1913, 83 elk from Yellowstone National Park were brought into the state; they are the foundation of today's populations.

ABOVE: Elk (female) and two calves **RIGHT:** Elk (male)

Mule deer (male, left, and female)

MULE DEER
Odocoileus hemionus

DESCRIPTION: Gray-tan overall, white throat and rump, black-tipped tail; oversized, mule-like ears move independently; males have antlers with main beams that split and branches that split again, spanning up to 4 feet

SIZE: Length of 4.5 to 7.5 feet, plus tail of 5 to 8 inches; height of 4 to 5.5 feet (including antlers); weight of 110 to 225 pounds; male larger than female

DIET: Shrubs, grasses, forbs and trees

HABITAT: Desert scrub, wooded grasslands, woodlands and forests, often near water

DISTRIBUTION: Statewide

■ Mule deer run with a stiff-legged gait called stotting. The principle family group consists of an older doe, her previous female offspring and youngsters (yearling males break away). Bucks form loose bachelor groups and compete during winter rut for breeding rights. After, antlers are shed as described for elk. Speckled fawns, born midsummer, are left hidden for four to eight weeks until sturdy enough to join the herd. New mothers usually give birth to singletons, while older does produce twins. Ungulates like mule deer are hunted by large predators: mountain lions, wolves, coyotes, bobcats, eagles ... and, of course, humans.

COUES WHITE-TAILED DEER
Odocoileus virginianus couesi

DESCRIPTION: Gray-brown overall; white around eyes, over muzzle and under hindquarters; long tail has fluffy white underside; male antlers have forward-curving beam with three or four tines
SIZE: Length of 3 to 6 feet, plus tail of 6 to 12 inches; height of up to 4 feet (including antlers); weight of 50 to 100 pounds; male larger than female
DIET: Shrubs, trees, grasses, forbs, agave, prickly pear cactuses and occasional crops
HABITAT: Primarily woodlands and riparian areas, but may range into grasslands and forests; 3,000 to 10,000 feet
DISTRIBUTION: Mogollon Rim and White Mountains down into Arizona's southeastern mountains
■ This diminutive subspecies, Arizona's only white-tailed deer, conceals itself amid trees. When the deer is alert to danger, its namesake tail is held erect like a white flag. Reproduction and family life are similar to mule deer. In addition to predation, drought is a significant cause of mortality in the Southwest. Deer rely heavily on smells, and white-tailed deer possess many glands for scent-marking, including a pair inside the rear legs, called tarsals, that emit a personalized aroma. Every step is marked by an odiferous, cheesy substance from glands between the hoof toes.

Coues white-tailed deer (male)

American pronghorns

AMERICAN PRONGHORN

Antilocapra americana

DESCRIPTION: Copper-colored with white sides, belly and rump; white markings on slender neck and face; short mane; both sexes have horns (female up to 4 inches, male 8 to 20 inches)

SIZE: Length of 4 to 5 feet, plus tail of 3 to 7 inches; height of up to 5 feet (including horns); weight of 75 to 130 pounds

DIET: Forbs, shrubs, grasses and cactuses
HABITAT: Semi-desert grasslands, other grasslands, open woodlands and forests
DISTRIBUTION: Pockets throughout the state

■ *Antilocapra* translates to "antelope-goat," but the pronghorn is actually neither. It forms its own taxonomic family, endemic to North America, and lives a nomadic, herd-based

life. As the continent's fastest land animal, the pronghorn can sprint up to 70 mph. If that seems like cheetah speeds, it's no coincidence: According to one theory, pronghorns' swiftness harks back to a bygone era when cheetah-like cats hunted them. Horns are described as bone cores covered with keratin sheaths. Normally they are permanent, but male pronghorns grow extra-long sheaths that are shed off the bone each year. Pronghorn breeding season (August and September) normally results in two fawns per female, born in spring. Except for nursing periods, fawns are left hidden and alone for the first week and weaned after about four months. **SIMILAR SPECIES:** The Sonoran pronghorn is an endangered subspecies that exists in two small populations (Southwestern Arizona and Mexico); the Chihuahuan, or Mexican, pronghorn is in the state's southeastern corner. Both are smaller and paler.

DESERT BIGHORN
Ovis canadensis nelsoni

DESCRIPTION: Gray-tan overall; white muzzle, rump and belly; both sexes have curved horns (female 10 to 13 inches, male 30 to 40 inches)
SIZE: Length of 4 to 6 feet, plus tail of 4 to 6 inches; height of up to 4.5 feet (including horns); weight of 75 to 225 pounds; male larger than female
DIET: Grasses, forbs and shrubs
HABITAT: Desert canyons, steep talus slopes and rocky buttes at all elevations; prefers open terrain with unobstructed views
DISTRIBUTION: Western Arizona and some of the southern region

■ In petroglyphs, bighorns symbolize Arizona's natural history. Adapted for high-cliff living, they possess exceptional depth perception and specialized feet. Hard outer hooves catch narrow (2-inch) rock protrusions, while soft inner pads cling to stone, allowing these skillful sheep to bound nearly 20 feet from ledge to ledge. Acute distance vision helps them identify predators from afar. While bighorns may be found foraging on level terrain, where edible plants grow best, they always are within reach of a steep safe haven. Adapted for the desert, they can go more than 10 days without water, even in summer. Maternal herds of five to 15 ewes remain within their natal range, but rams travel greater distances. Their massive horns portray status. Unlike antlers, horns are permanent, and a high-ranking male's may curl

Desert bighorn (male)

full circle. Autumn rut brings head-to-head combat with reverberating *cracks* that can be heard for a mile. The champion breeds. Pregnancy lasts about six months and produces one lamb per ewe. Young are vulnerable to coyotes, mountain lions and golden eagles, but those that survive may live 10 years or longer.
SIMILAR SPECIES: The Rocky Mountain bighorn (east-central and northeast) is larger and slightly darker.

Desert bighorns (adolescents)

COLLARED PECCARY or JAVELINA
Pecari tajacu

DESCRIPTION: Rotund; bristly hair is black, tan and white; faint buff "collar" at shoulder; triangular head; pig-like snout; tips of canine teeth (tusks) may be visible; short, thin legs with split hooves
SIZE: Length of 2.5 to 3.5 feet, plus tail of 1 to 2 inches; height of 1.5 to 2 feet; weight of 30 to 65 pounds
DIET: Mostly prickly pear cactuses; some mesquite pods, fruits, roots and animal matter
HABITAT: Desert scrub, canyons, woodlands and suburban areas, always within range of water
DISTRIBUTION: Most of southern half of state and parts of the Grand Canyon

■ Despite their basic appearance, these are *not* pigs. Pigs came from Europe. Peccaries originated in South America and ranged northward. This species, which subsequently arrived in the American Southwest, has become an iconic desert animal known as the javelina (its sharp tusks resemble spear-like weapons called javelins). Javelinas travel in family herds of six to 30 individuals. Predominantly crepuscular, they forage as they roam, and scent glands on their rumps secrete a potent, oily musk to mark territory and keep the herd together. Baby javelinas are called reds because of their rusty-brown color — the herd's dominant male fathers most of them. Following a 145-day gestation, a mother delivers two reds weighing but a pound each. Precocial, they follow her like ducklings, protected by the entire herd. With terrible eyesight and no speed to outrun predators such as mountain lions and bobcats, a javelina's main protection is its 1- to 2-inch tusks. Adults will readily charge intruders while rapidly clacking their teeth. In quiet times, these social animals groom each other and softly vocalize. Days are spent lounging in cave-like shelters or patches of shade.

LIVING WITH WILDLIFE

With such inadequate vision, javelinas are easily startled and may respond with defensive aggression, especially when reds are present. They are not seeking a fight and just need space to move away. Step back. Keep dogs leashed. Javelinas love to gobble freshly planted spring flowers and Halloween pumpkins left unattended. Discourage their visits by removing edibles, including fallen fruit and garbage, from your yard. Don't dismay; it's a reasonable concession for the luxury of living near such marvelous wildlife.

ABOVE: Collared peccaries (reds) **RIGHT:** Collared peccary (adult)

Lesser long-nosed bat

BATS

Bats are misunderstood, irrationally feared and unjustly persecuted. They comprise the second-largest mammal order in the world, behind rodents: *Chiroptera*. Derived from Greek, it means "hand-wing." Elongated hand bones are covered by membranous skin, which stretches between fingers and connects arms to legs (tail, too, if present). Clawed thumbs jut forward. With these hand-wings, bats are the only mammals that can truly fly. In North America, there are four chiropteran families, all nocturnal: *Phyllostomidae* (leaf-nosed bats), *Vespertilionidae* (evening bats, most common), *Molossidae* (free-tailed bats) and *Mormoopidae* (leaf-chinned bats, rare in U.S.). Arizona has 28 bat species — as many as New Mexico, and more than any other state except Texas —and all are beneficial to humans. Two eat primarily nectar and pollen, and are pollinators that play a vital role in desert ecology. The rest are insectivores, offering free, organic pest control. Plus, gardeners know bat excrement (guano) makes outstanding fertilizer! Contrary to fable, bats are not blind. Most have excellent vision further augmented by echolocation. By making high-frequency chirps (up to 200 per second) and listening for the reverberating sound waves (sonar), a sensory image is produced. Because Arizona bats' chirps are vocally emitted, bats often fly with mouth agape. Daylight finds them clinging to roofs of caves, buildings or crevices. They can sleep upside-down without falling because their forward-facing hind feet reflexively clench and must be deliberately released. Bats are also the only mammals with delayed fertilization. Several months may pass after mating before females ovulate and become pregnant. Actual gestation lasts an average of 40 days, and most species deliver just one pup. In spring and summer, mothers assemble maternity colonies (sometimes in the thousands) to raise young while males roost alone or in small groups. Pups may be carried the first days but then are left in a community nursery area called a crèche. They fly by three to eight weeks of age and stay with their mothers until survival skills are learned. Most Arizona bats either migrate south or hibernate in winter, although some stay and remain active. Due to low reproductive rates and sensitivity to disruption, many bat populations are in steep decline and must be carefully managed through conservation strategies.

LIVING WITH WILDLIFE

Help urban wildlife by voicing support for bat-friendly structures on bridges. If a bat is found on the ground, it is likely to be sick and may pose a health risk — do not touch it, and keep dogs and children away. Gently place a box over the animal and call a wildlife-rehabilitation center (page 152) or the Arizona Game and Fish Department for assistance.

LESSER LONG-NOSED BAT
Leptonycteris yerbabuenae

DESCRIPTION: Dense, cinnamon-gray fur; elongated snout; leaf-like projection sticks up from nose; triangular ears are moderately sized; no visible tail
SIZE: Length of 3 to 3.5 inches; wingspan of 12 to 14 inches
DIET: Nectar, pollen and fruit of columnar cactuses and agaves
HABITAT: Desert scrub, grasslands and hillsides

DISTRIBUTION: Southeastern Arizona
CONSERVATION STATUS: Endangered
■ If lesser long-nosed bats disappear, so will the pollination of fundamental desert plants like the giant saguaro. As this keystone species hovers to lap nectar from night-blooming flowers with its specialized 3-inch tongue, pollen collects on its fur and is carried substantial distances between cactuses. And ingested seeds, disseminated in packets of yellow guano, cultivate new plant growth. Echolocation is poorly developed in these bats, and food is located mainly by sight.
SIMILAR SPECIES: The Mexican long-tongued bat (only extreme south) is more gray.

Arizona myotis

ARIZONA MYOTIS
Myotis occultus

DESCRIPTION: Fluffy; tan to copper-brown, with darker face and wings; pointed snout; wide-spread ears; small eyes; distinctively long hind feet
SIZE: Length of 2 to 2.5 inches, plus tail of about 1.5 inches; wingspan of 8.5 to 10.5 inches
DIET: Mostly flying aquatic insects (can eat 600 mosquitoes an hour)

HABITAT: Woodlands, forests (roosts under bark of ponderosa-pine snags) and desert-riparian and urban areas, almost always near water
DISTRIBUTION: Most of Arizona, except far north and far south
■ The Arizona myotis is just one of many "evening bats." It tends to fly erratically and may be seen before dusk, foraging over water, frequently netting prey out of the air with its flight membranes. Since it also skims insects off the water surface and risks accidentally tumbling in, this bat can swim. The species is long-lived, and an individual may survive to 30 years.
SIMILAR SPECIES: There are nine myotis species in Arizona, but the Yuma myotis (statewide) may be particularly difficult to distinguish.

MEXICAN FREE-TAILED BAT
Tadarida brasiliensis mexicana

DESCRIPTION: Gray-brown fur with darker face and wings; wrinkled upper lip; wide ears; tail extends beyond rear flight membranes
SIZE: Length of 2 to 2.5 inches, plus tail of 1.5 to 2 inches; wingspan of 10 to 12 inches

Mexican free-tailed bats

Pallid bat

DIET: Flying insects (especially moths)
HABITAT: Desert scrub, canyons, woodlands, forests, and agricultural and urban areas
DISTRIBUTION: Statewide in summer; small population hibernates in south through winter

■ From March to October, the Mexican free-tailed bat is Arizona's most abundant bat. Enormous colonies roost in caves or crevices and may share space with pallid bats. Amazingly, a mother can recognize her pup's vocalizations and scent among tens of thousands of clustered bodies.

PALLID BAT
Antrozous pallidus

DESCRIPTION: Pale beige above and cream below; salmon-colored facial skin; huge, grayish ears; piggish nose; long tail held within flight membranes

SIZE: Length of 2 to 3.5 inches, plus tail of 1.5 to 2 inches; wingspan of 14 to 16 inches
DIET: Ground-dwelling invertebrates (including scorpions and centipedes)
HABITAT: Desert scrub, canyons, grasslands, woodlands and open forests
DISTRIBUTION: Statewide

■ Pallid bats are unique because they feed primarily on the ground. They actually hear the footfalls of insects and effectively crawl over rocks and branches to capture prey. To avoid hungry mammals, snakes and amphibians themselves, the bats rarely devour their quarry on the spot but carry it to an elevated roost for consumption. Strangely, males may be present in maternity colonies, which generally number about 20 bats but can number more than 100. This species has glands behind its nostrils that secrete a skunky scent. It makes several sounds, including buzzes, clicks and high-pitched notes.

📷 JOE COELHO

LIVING WITH WILDLIFE

Would you like to witness an evening emergence of Mexican free-tailed bats? During summer, they can be observed in Phoenix, departing the flood-control tunnel next to the Arizona Canal near 40th Street and Camelback Road. In Tucson, they take flight from under the bridge at Campbell Avenue and East River Road. In the Southern Arizona ghost town of Ruby, they stream skyward (pictured) from an old mine shaft. *Quietly* arrive before sunset and enjoy the twilight spectacle.

VIRGINIA OPOSSUM
Didelphis virginiana californica

DESCRIPTION: Grizzled charcoal gray and white; long, pointed head and snout; large, rounded ears; bead-like eyes; hairless tail; back foot has opposable thumb; pouch on abdomen
SIZE: Length of 13 to 22 inches, plus tail of 10 to 20 inches; weight of 3 to 13 pounds
DIET: Carrion, small animals, eggs, fruits and plant matter
HABITAT: Woodlands and riparian and urban areas
DISTRIBUTION: Huachuca and Pajarito mountains of Southeastern Arizona

▪ People often are surprised that opossums inhabit Arizona, although they are extremely rare. The Virginia opossum is North America's only marsupial, and the Mexican subspecies that ranges into Arizona, *el tlacuache*, appears darker in color than the eastern variety. What a curious creature! Its prehensile tail offers balance but, despite myth, is too weak to hang from for any duration. So the animals sleep in leafy log hollows or abandoned burrows. A female may have two or three litters a year. After a mere 13-day pregnancy, up to 23 pea-sized joeys endeavor to climb from birth canal to pouch. Only about eight manage the journey. They crawl inside to nurse and grow for approximately eight weeks, then ride on their mother's back for several more weeks before dispersing. Mortality is high, with a life span around two years. Few joeys survive to independence, and adults face numerous nocturnal predators. While the opossum's normal defense includes hissing and teeth-baring, if a threat becomes too stressful, physiological shock may ensue. It's a peculiar trick of nature, feigning death — not only does the body collapse stock-still, mouth open, tongue lolling, but the gums turn gray and anal glands ooze the smell of decay. Many predators are repulsed or lose interest.

BLACK BEAR
Ursus americanus

DESCRIPTION: Bulky body; dense fur of varying color (black, brown, rust or blond); long muzzle is lighter in color; rounded ears; small eyes; short, inconspicuous tail
SIZE: Length of 4 to 6 feet, plus tail of 3 to 5 inches; height of 3 to 3.5 feet; weight of 200 to 600 pounds; male larger than female
DIET: Omnivorous; berries, grasses, roots, honeycomb, insects, fish, small mammals and refuse
HABITAT: Forests, woodlands and occasionally urban areas, from 4,000 to 10,000 feet; attracted to food at campgrounds and trash dumps
DISTRIBUTION: Central and East-Central Arizona, plus pockets in north, northeast and southeast

▪ *Carnivora* seems an unlikely order for black bears, which eat 80 percent plant matter. Their name is misleading, too, since they are not always black. Active from April to October, they

Virginia opossum

Black bear

are generally solitary and can be active day or night but are crepuscular in areas frequented by humans. While infrequently observed, over-turned rocks and deep scratches in tree bark are telltale signs of their presence. Summers are spent gorging food, and bears may travel 100 miles or farther and/or enter atypical habitats in search of good fare. Breeding also takes place in summer. Although seven months pass before birth, actual gestation is only two to three months. Bears exhibit delayed implantation, a multi-month pause in the development of the embryo (not to be confused with delayed fer-tilization in bats). Cubs, usually two, are born in a winter den and raised by a protective mother. Nursing lasts about seven months; however, cubs enjoy parental care until just over 1.5 years of age. Black bears excel at swimming and climbing, and even with a lumbering gait, they can reach 30 mph in short bursts.

Mountain lion

MOUNTAIN LION or COUGAR or PUMA
Puma concolor

DESCRIPTION: Tawny overall, buff below; relatively small head; long tail may be dark at tip; young (up to 6 months) are spotted; may resemble bobcats, but lack ear tufts and bobbed tails

SIZE: Length of 3 to 5 feet, plus tail of 2 to 3 feet; height of 2 to 3 feet; weight of 70 to 150 pounds; male larger than female

DIET: Mostly deer; also bighorn sheep, javelinas and some small mammals (including rabbits, porcupines and raccoons)

HABITAT: Desert scrub, canyons, grasslands, woodlands and forests; prefers rugged terrain with woody cover; home range can be up to 150 square miles

DISTRIBUTION: Statewide

■ Cats are true carnivores. They belong to the family *Felidae* and possess retractable claws, which never wear down. When the claws are drawn in, furred feet stalk in silence. When extended, sharp points form lethal daggers. The mountain lion primarily hunts around dusk and dawn. As an ambush predator, it easily climbs trees and boulders to gain advantage and can leap 20 feet onto unsuspecting prey. A single deer provides a week or two of meals; leftovers are buried between feedings. Males mark territory with urine and turn trees into scratching posts. Breeding may occur any season, and a female gives birth to three or four helpless cubs in a secluded natal den. They are weaned after five to six weeks and depart the den after six to nine weeks but stay with their mother up to two years. Like African lions, when a male mountain lion overtakes a territory, he may kill existing cubs to instill his own genetic line. Mountain lions, despite their size, cannot roar. Instead, they hiss, growl or caterwaul like house cats. Although these elusive cats avoid urban areas and humans in general, occasional conflicts have been reported.

BOBCAT
Lynx rufus baileyi

DESCRIPTION: Cinnamon or gray-tan with dark spots, white below; tufted black ears with white behind; ruffed cheeks; short legs; characteristically "bobbed" (approximately 6 inches) tail
SIZE: Length of 2 to 3.5 feet, plus tail of 4 to 8 inches; height of 1.5 to 2.5 feet; weight of 14 to 30 pounds; male larger than female
DIET: Mostly rabbits; some rodents; occasional birds, lizards, snakes and carrion

HABITAT: Almost all Arizona habitats, including suburban areas; home range can be up to 12 square miles
DISTRIBUTION: Statewide

■ Also called a wildcat, this is the mascot for the University of Arizona. This solitary and crepuscular hunter waits motionless, masked by camouflage, and then rushes passing rabbits. Extra food is cached under bits of leaf litter. With superb night vision, the bobcat easily travels through darkness and is capable of jumping 12 feet. During breeding season (February and March), territorial males can be heard yowling as they pursue multiple females. Up to seven cubs (two or three, on average) are born after a 63-day gestation period. The mother retains alternative dens and may relocate her broods. Cubs' eyes open at around 10 days, and the cubs start learning to hunt after eight weeks. By a year of age, they are on their own. As does a house cat, a bobcat commonly covers its scat with scratched dirt or debris. It also purrs when content (mountain lions purr, too).

Bobcat

MEXICAN GRAY WOLF
Canis lupus baileyi

DESCRIPTION: Grizzled yellow-gray fur tinged with black; bushy tail; long legs; may appear similar to coyote, but weight, facial features and gait are distinct

SIZE: Smallest subspecies of gray wolf, with length of 3.5 to 4 feet, plus tail of 11 to 18 inches; height of 25 to 32 inches; weight of 50 to 80 pounds; male larger than female

DIET: Primarily elk; some other ungulates; occasional small prey, plant matter and livestock

HABITAT: Forests, woodlands and grasslands; prefers montane habitat around 6,000 feet; home range of about 200 square miles

DISTRIBUTION: Mexican Wolf Experimental Population Area in Central to East-Central Arizona and West-Central New Mexico

CONSERVATION STATUS: Endangered (retains status even though *Canis lupus* is delisted)

■ The Mexican gray wolf, *el lobo*, is one of the rarest mammals in the world. Originally ranging throughout the southwestern U.S. and Mexico, this native species was pushed to the brink of extinction — a victim of guns, traps and poisons. Between 1977 and 1980, the last few wild Mexican gray wolves were brought into captivity to start a

Mexican gray wolf

LIVING WITH WILDLIFE

Coyotes generally pose no danger to humans, but food should never be placed within their reach. (This holds true for black bears, too!) The majority of bites and other negative interactions occur when natural fears are diminished through a pattern of feeding. More often than not, the animal is put to death as the result of an adverse encounter.

Coyote

breeding program. Reintroduction to Arizona habitat began in 1998, and under careful management, the state's population has slowly risen. These canids live in social packs of two to 10 individuals. They exhibit complex interactions and communicate with a variety of vocalizations, including their spine-tingling howl. In April, the alpha female delivers a litter of two to eight pups. Young remain in the den for the first three weeks of life before meeting other members of the pack. Life span in the wild is usually less than 10 years. Studies have shown apex predators such as wolves can be critical to ecological strength and stability.

COYOTE
Canis latrans mearnsi

DESCRIPTION: Thin-framed; grizzled gray-tan fur; pointed ears; long nose; low-slung, black-tipped tail
SIZE: Length of 3 to 3.5 feet, plus tail of 12 to 14 inches; height of 18 to 24 inches; weight of 19 to 30 pounds
DIET: Mostly rabbits, rodents, birds, reptiles, insects and some offspring of large mammals (including deer, pronghorns and bighorns); occasional carrion, fruits, grasses and refuse
HABITAT: Desert scrub, grasslands, broken forests and urban areas
DISTRIBUTION: Statewide
■ Coyotes are long-distance runners, traveling day or night. Unlike wolves, they do not live in packs, although two or more may socialize or hunt together. Their yipping calls are a familiar evening sound. During breeding season (January to March), coyotes form monogamous pairs and the female excavates or overtakes a den. By spring, four to eight pups are born. Life span in the wild is normally six to eight years. Although coyotes range across most of the contiguous United States, they remain a traditional desert species, one that plays a central role in American Indian folklore and elicits a broad range of emotions.

Gray fox

GRAY FOX

Urocyon cinereoargenteus scottii

DESCRIPTION: Plush fur is salt-and-pepper above and white below; rufous cheeks and sides; fluffy tail has dark dorsal stripe
SIZE: Length of 1.5 to 2 feet, plus tail of 10 to 17 inches; height of about 1.5 feet; weight of 5.5 to 13 pounds
DIET: More omnivorous than other foxes; rabbits, rodents, birds, invertebrates, fruits, berries, nuts, grasses and carrion
HABITAT: Woodlands, forests, grasslands, desert scrub, riparian areas and urban areas; prefers rugged terrain with wooded cover
DISTRIBUTION: Statewide

■ Gray foxes can do something other canids cannot: climb trees. Although predominantly nocturnal, rare sightings do occur on overcast or winter days. And the scream-like calls of mating pairs can be heard during breeding season (January to March). The female, although capable of digging a den, usually just assumes a rock crevice, abandoned burrow or elevated tree hollow where she gives birth to one litter of two to seven pups in April or May. The father helps with pup-rearing by bringing food to the den, and extra food may be cached outside in shallow holes marked with urine. Pups are weaned by 10 weeks and begin foraging on their own after three to four months. Gray foxes are susceptible to diseases such as rabies and distemper. And they are still trapped for their soft fur.

SIMILAR SPECIES: The kit fox (Sonoran, Mohave and Chihuahuan deserts, plus parts of northeast) has a lanky body, enormous ears and a black-tipped tail. The red fox (extreme northern edge of state) has a white-tipped tail.

RINGTAIL

Bassariscus astutus

DESCRIPTION: Cat-like shape; golden fur tinged with black; buff belly; long tail has bold black and white bands; dark eyes circled with white fur; lacks black mask of the raccoon and long snout of the coati

SIZE: Length of 10 to 14 inches, plus tail of 10 to 14 inches; weight of about 2 pounds

DIET: Small vertebrates (especially rodents), invertebrates and fruits (including prickly pear)

HABITAT: Desert scrub, canyons, talus slopes, grasslands, woodlands, forests and urban areas (sometimes inside human dwellings); prefers rocky areas with water nearby

DISTRIBUTION: Statewide, except flatlands and highest elevations

■ The nickname "miner's cat" is confusing because this is no feline: The ringtail is related to the raccoon (as is the coati). It was designated Arizona's state mammal in 1986. Because ringtails are strictly nocturnal and secretive by nature, only the luckiest night hikers will glimpse one in their headlamps. Days are spent sleeping in a den — a tree hollow or underground burrow — sometimes lined with soft grass or leaves. This first-rate climber can rotate its hind feet 180 degrees (like a tree squirrel), allowing the ringtail to descend vertical surfaces headfirst. A pouncing hunter, it delivers a deadly bite to the neck. Spring mating produces a litter of one to four kits born in May or June. For almost a month, the kits consume nothing but milk, and their ear flaps droop until six weeks of age. By two to three months, they begin foraging with their mother. Great horned owls are the ringtail's principal predator, but coyotes and bobcats also pose a threat.

Ringtail

COMMON RACCOON
Procyon lotor

DESCRIPTION: Dense fur, grizzled gray-brown above and white below; bushy tail (shorter than ringtail's) is banded pale ochre and black; distinctive black mask covers eyes and cheeks; lacks elongated snout of the coati
SIZE: Length of 1.5 to 2 feet, plus tail of 8 to 12 inches; weight of 12 to 35 pounds
DIET: Opportunistic omnivore; plant matter, invertebrates (including crayfish, grubs and larvae), small vertebrates (including fish and amphibians), eggs, carrion and refuse
HABITAT: Nearly all Arizona habitats where water and cover are available, including urban areas
DISTRIBUTION: Scattered statewide

■ Raccoons are nocturnal riparian scavengers, so muddy tracks give them away. Their long back feet juxtapose small hands, each with five dexterous fingers sensitized for feeling around in water and manipulating food. While tree hollows are preferred for sleeping, any reasonable location will do. Several raccoons may gather in a winter den, but they do not hibernate, just sleep. During breeding season (February and March), the male, weirdly called a boar, may roam miles in search of females, called sows. After mating, he is driven away and does not help with the rearing of offspring. An average of three or four kits, born in April or May, are weaned by late summer. Because these adaptable problem-solvers learn by emulating their mother, they often stay with her until the next litter arrives. Cornered raccoons are extremely aggressive. Ears pinned back, they snarl and growl. They have the same predators as ringtails but are also frequently hit by cars while crossing darkened roads. Life expectancy, at best, is less than five years in the wild.

Common raccoon

White-nosed coati

WHITE-NOSED COATI or COATIMUNDI — *Nasua narica*

DESCRIPTION: Dense fur, reddish brown overall and white around eyes and muzzle; long claws on front feet; elongated snout and muted tail bands distinguish from ringtail and raccoon

SIZE: Length of 1.5 to 2 feet, plus tail of 17 to 26 inches; weight of 8 to 20 pounds; male larger than female

DIET: Mostly invertebrates and fruits; some small vertebrates and eggs; occasional crops

HABITAT: Forests, woodlands, wooded canyons and grasslands; usually near water

DISTRIBUTION: Central, East-Central and Southeastern Arizona

■ *Nasua* derives from the Latin word *nasus*, meaning "nose" — the coatimundi's is certainly prominent. Unlike ringtails and raccoons, coatis are diurnal and social. Loose bands of up to 20 females may travel together, bushy tails poking skyward. They spend much of the day sniffing, scratching and rooting for foodstuffs but do not work cooperatively or share meals. Nights are passed asleep in the trees. Males are solitary except for mating (reported to be April in Arizona). Pregnancy lasts about 75 days, and a mother separates from her band to build a natal den where she bears three to six young. As they nurse, she communicates with them through soft chatters and purrs. The expanded family will rejoin the band within about six weeks.

American badger

AMERICAN BADGER
Taxidea taxus

DESCRIPTION: Short, wide stance; grizzled gray-tan above, buff below; black feet with thick claws; light and dark facial markings, with bold white stripe through center of head and nape
SIZE: Length of 1.5 to 2.5 feet, plus tail of 4 to 6 inches; weight of 8 to 26 pounds; male larger than female
DIET: Carnivore; rodents, rabbits, birds, eggs, snakes, frogs and invertebrates
HABITAT: Desert scrub, grasslands, montane meadows and fields; prefers open terrain
DISTRIBUTION: Statewide
■ Badgers, along with otters and ferrets, are in the weasel family (*Mustelidae*). These powerful diggers easily tunnel after rodents and snakes, further excavating the holes into large subterranean burrows (up to 30 feet long and 10 feet deep). Dirt, fur and bones mark an elliptical den entrance 8 to 12 inches wide. Although these solitary hunters do not hibernate, they infrequently emerge during winter months. Delayed implantation affects their reproductive cycle, with late-summer breeding resulting in litters of one to five cubs born in March or April. Reputed for their ferocious nature, adults are quick to attack, especially if protecting cubs.

BLACK-FOOTED FERRET
Mustela nigripes

DESCRIPTION: Tubular shape; yellow-buff fur tinged with brown; light belly; legs and tip of tail black-brown; white face with black mask
SIZE: Length of 15 to 18 inches, plus tail of 5 to 6 inches; weight of 1.5 to 2.5 pounds
DIET: Almost exclusively prairie dogs
HABITAT: Grasslands; resides in prairie-dog burrows
DISTRIBUTION: Established in Aubrey Valley in Northwestern Arizona; recently introduced on private lands north of Williams in Central Arizona
CONSERVATION STATUS: Endangered
■ A 1930s poisoning campaign exterminated Gunnison's prairie dogs, perceived as competition for cattle land. There was a secondary casualty: the black-footed ferret. When the nation's last known ferret died in 1979, the species was declared extinct. But in 1981, a relic colony was discovered, and eventually its last living members — 18 total — were collected for captive breeding. Arizona launched reintroductions in 1996, and wild-born kits are steadily increasing. Black-footed ferrets are solitary, except for mating (March and April) and when females are caring for young. After a 42-day pregnancy, a mother nurses three to five kits, which become independent by fall. This nocturnal predator's keen sense of smell aids its subterranean travels. The black-footed ferret has few natural enemies but is prone to disease, and its short life expectancy (one to three years in the wild) is a challenge for

LIVING WITH WILDLIFE
Every spring and fall, qualified volunteers assist the Arizona Game and Fish Department's black-footed-ferret project with overnight spotlighting surveys in Aubrey Valley. It is an opportunity to see a critically endangered species and personally aid in its recovery. If you are interested in participating, details can be found online at www.azgfd.gov.

Black-footed ferret

population management.
SIMILAR SPECIES: The long-tailed weasel (Mogollon Rim, "sky islands" and parts of Northeastern Arizona) is smaller, cinnamon above and white below.

NORTH AMERICAN RIVER OTTER
Lontra canadensis

DESCRIPTION: Elongated body; fur appears oily; brown overall, with silvery throat and belly; flattened head; thick, tapering tail; webbed feet
SIZE: Length of 2 to 2.5 feet, plus tail of 12 to 20 inches; weight of 11 to 31 pounds
DIET: Fish and invasive crawfish; some vertebrates and insects
HABITAT: Permanent riparian areas with ample prey
DISTRIBUTION: Verde River corridor of Central Arizona

■ Otters in Arizona? Yes. The state's native subspecies, *L.c. sonora*, historically inhabited all major tributaries of the Colorado and Gila rivers, but most, possibly all, populations are extirpated.

Another subspecies, *L.c. lataxina*, was introduced to the Verde River corridor from 1981 to 1983 and has successfully reproduced. This semi-aquatic mammal can hold its breath for up to eight minutes. It uses or builds dens near the riverbank, some with underwater entrances leading to leaf-lined chambers. The female raises her offspring alone, normally one to three pups born in spring after about eight months' delayed implantation. Her family is playfully swimming together within three months.

Northern American river otter

TOP: GEORGE ANDREJKO, ARIZONA GAME AND FISH DEPARTMENT   ABOVE: PEGGY COLEMAN

Western spotted skunk

WESTERN SPOTTED SKUNK
Spilogale gracilis

DESCRIPTION: Slender build; black with several white spots, bars or stripes; white-tipped tail has cascading hair

SIZE: Arizona's smallest skunk, with length of 9 to 12 inches, plus tail of 4 to 7 inches; weight of 7 to 30 ounces

DIET: Mostly rodents; some lizards, birds and insects; occasional plant matter

HABITAT: Desert scrub with riparian areas, grasslands, woodlands and agricultural areas; prefers rocky terrain

DISTRIBUTION: Statewide

▪ This unique-looking mouser is surprisingly widespread in Arizona. It is strictly nocturnal, faster than other skunks and an adept tree climber. Mating occurs in September and October, but like black bears, Western spotted skunks have delayed implantation, so even though gestation is 50 to 60 days, young (two to four) are not born until the following April or May. When threatened, the skunk stomps its feet in warning and raises into a handstand. Pushed, it employs notoriously foul-smelling anal glands, accurately spraying intruders up to 10 feet away. Skunks are susceptible to rabies, and those that have contracted the disease may act tame or confused.

SIMILAR SPECIES: The striped skunk (statewide) is more common, larger and with two white dorsal stripes. The hognose skunk (west-central to southeast) has a broad dorsal stripe from head to tail. The hooded skunk (south-central and southeast) is like the hognose but has a tiny stripe between its eyes.

AMERICAN BEAVER
Castor canadensis

DESCRIPTION: Rotund; coarse, oily fur; dark tan to brown; flat, paddle-shaped tail; webbed hind feet

SIZE: North America's largest rodent, with length of 2 to 3 feet, plus tail of 8 to 14 inches; weight of 30 to 70 pounds

DIET: Herbivorous; tree bark, leaves, roots and aquatic plants

HABITAT: Montane streams, forest lakes and wooded desert-riparian areas

DISTRIBUTION: Statewide; parts of Colorado, Lower Colorado, Verde, Gila and San Pedro river zones and certain smaller tributaries

▪ Working night shifts, this semi-aquatic rodent gnaws through tree trunks and uses the felled lumber, along with twigs, grass and mud, to build (or repair) a giant, dome-shaped dam. The inside den, called a lodge, is entered from beneath the water surface. These environmental engineers have a profound impact on their

RANDALL D. BABB, ARIZONA GAME AND FISH DEPARTMENT

American beaver

habitat, but in general, flood damage caused by beaver dams is offset by the creation of new wetlands. Indeed, studies confirm richer abundance of bird life along waterways inhabited by beavers. Beavers are colonial, and each mating pair shares a lodge. A mother normally delivers three or four kits in spring after a four-month pregnancy. Just a week later, the kits can swim. Despite a waddling gait on land, these rodents are quite graceful in water, and adults can hold their breath for 15 minutes. When submerged, thin, transparent tissues called nictitating membranes — nature's swimming goggles — cover the beavers' eyes. Loud tail slaps on water are used for communication.

SIMILAR SPECIES: The muskrat (parts of Colorado, Little Colorado and Gila river basins) is significantly smaller (about 12 inches) with a long, narrow tail.

NORTH AMERICAN PORCUPINE
Erethizon dorsatum

DESCRIPTION: Hunched posture; chocolate-brown hairs and long, yellowish quills on back, sides and tail; small, dark eyes and ears; long claws
SIZE: Length of 20 to 26 inches, plus tail of 8 to 10 inches; weight of 11 to 30 pounds
DIET: Tree bark, stems, leaves, flowers, berries and sometimes wooden buildings or tools
HABITAT: Forests, woodlands and some desert scrub with associated riparian areas
DISTRIBUTION: Statewide, except parts of southwest

■ The porcupine carries a mighty shield of protection — more than 30,000 needle-like quills. These modified hairs are not projectiles but will readily pierce skin with the briefest of contact. As confrontation is preferably avoided, a threatened porcupine will chatter its teeth and emit a pungent musk as fair warning. Unheeded, the defensive rodent lashes its tail and can drive its quills extremely deep. Skillful hunters, such as mountain lions and eagles, that accomplish a kill may die later from infected punctures. Obviously, porcupine mating must be consensual. Breeding takes place in autumn or early winter, and after a seven-month pregnancy, one baby is born in spring. Unlike most rodent babies, which are born pink and blind, a porcupette (that's what baby porcupines are called) enters the world with eyes open, sporting tiny, soft quills and budding teeth. It will be on its own in just five months. These animals den in tree hollows, caves or burrows, and rest on branches. Nocturnal, nearsighted and sluggish afoot, they often are hit by cars on dark roadways.

North American porcupine

SQUIRRELS

Squirrels are a family (*Sciuridae*) of small, slender, bushy-tailed rodents. Like all members of *Rodentia*, they have long, paired incisors that grow throughout their lives. Seeds, nuts, fruits and other plant matter make up the majority of their diet, but they also may eat insects, small animals and even carrion. Ground squirrels tend to be more omnivorous. They live in chambered subterranean burrows, while tree squirrels build arboreal nests called dreys. Most squirrels are diurnal or crepuscular. Births typically occur in springtime (sometimes fall, too), but length of gestation (three to six weeks) and litter size (three to 12 babies) vary by species. Although silent most of the time, they may chirp, trill or whistle — some stomp their feet — to announce danger. All of Arizona's squirrel species are hunted by birds, mammals and snakes.

CHIRICAHUA FOX SQUIRREL
Sciurus nayaritensis chiricahuae

DESCRIPTION: Grizzled reddish gray above; ochre belly and sides; round, short ears; bushy tail turns darker gray in winter
SIZE: Length of 11 to 13 inches, plus tail of 10 to 11 inches; weight of about 1.75 pounds
DIET: Mainly pine and Douglas-fir seeds, mistletoe berries and fungi
HABITAT: Canyons with pine-oak forest around 5,200 feet
DISTRIBUTION: Chiricahua Mountains of extreme Southeastern Arizona
■ The elusive Chiricahua fox squirrel is considered arboreal but spends a lot of time on the ground. It is active year-round and, unlike other tree squirrels, does not cache food.

Chiricahua fox squirrel

📷 GEORGE ANDREJKO, ARIZONA GAME AND FISH DEPARTMENT

Abert's squirrel

ABERT'S SQUIRREL
Sciurus aberti

DESCRIPTION: Body and tail are grizzled gray above, white below; coppery patch on back; long ears (1.75 inches with winter tufts); fluffy tail

SIZE: Length of 10 to 12 inches, plus tail of 8 to 10 inches; weight of 1.5 to 2 pounds

DIET: Ponderosa seeds, inner bark, buds and flowers; some fungi, bones and antlers

HABITAT: Ponderosa-pine forests above 6,000 feet

DISTRIBUTION: Kaibab Plateau (northwest) and Mogollon Rim to East-Central Arizona

■ This tree dweller is also called the tassel-eared squirrel. It is solitary except during courtship and uses ponderosa pines for nesting and food.

SIMILAR SPECIES: The Kaibab squirrel, *S. a. kaibabensis*, is a subspecies endemic to the North Rim of the Grand Canyon; it's distinguished by a blackish belly and an all-white tail.

ROCK SQUIRREL
Otospermophilus variegatus

DESCRIPTION: Grizzled gray-brown; white eye ring; long, semi-bushy tail
SIZE: Arizona's largest ground squirrel, with length of 11 to 13 inches, plus tail of 6 to 8 inches; weight of 1 to 2 pounds
DIET: Buds, seeds, insects, fruits, eggs, small animals and carrion
HABITAT: Rocky areas, talus slopes, oak-juniper canyons and roadside hills
DISTRIBUTION: Statewide except extreme southwestern corner
▪ Rock squirrels often live colonially with a dominant male. Although mostly found among rocks, they sometimes climb in trees and bushes. Litters are born from April to August.

Harris' antelope squirrel

Rock squirrel

HARRIS' ANTELOPE SQUIRREL
Ammospermophilus harrisii

DESCRIPTION: Rusty gray-brown with white stripe on each side; bushy gray tail, often arched over back; resembles a chipmunk, but lacks facial stripes
SIZE: Length of 6 to 7 inches, plus tail of 2.5 to 3.5 inches; weight of 4 to 5.5 ounces
DIET: Cactus fruits, cactus flowers, leaves, seeds and insects
HABITAT: Desert scrub and grasslands; dry, sparse rocky areas
DISTRIBUTION: West-Central and Southern Arizona
▪ This ground squirrel absorbs moisture from its food and is equipped with cheek pouches for carrying stores. It may be seen climbing cactuses.
SIMILAR SPECIES: The tail of the white-tailed antelope squirrel (north) is white underneath.

ROUND-TAILED GROUND SQUIRREL
Xerospermophilus tereticaudus

DESCRIPTION: Reddish gray-tan; white eye ring; tiny ears; long, thin tail; resembles a miniature prairie dog
SIZE: Length of 6.5 to 7 inches, plus tail of 2.5 to 4.5 inches; weight of 4 to 6.5 ounces
DIET: Mostly plants, seeds and insects
HABITAT: Desert scrub, sandy flats,

Round-tailed ground squirrel

grasslands and urban areas
DISTRIBUTION: More than a third of Arizona, toward the southwest
▪ This species normally lives in small, interactive colonies.
SIMILAR SPECIES: The spotted ground squirrel (most of the state, but uncommonly seen) has white speckles.

CLIFF CHIPMUNK
Tamias dorsalis

DESCRIPTION: Gray-brown and rust above, with one distinct, dark dorsal stripe and other fainter ones; pale belly; two bold, white stripes on each side of face; long, fluffy gray tail
SIZE: Length of 4.5 to 5.5 inches, plus tail of 3.5 to 5 inches; weight of about 2.5 ounces; female larger than male
DIET: Mostly nuts, seeds, fruits and flowers
HABITAT: Woodlands, forests and riparian areas; near cliffs and rocky outcrops
DISTRIBUTION: Mountain regions from northwest, angling diagonally into Southeastern Arizona
▪ Chipmunks are best known for packing their cheeks with food. Indeed, fully extended cheek pouches nearly equal the size of the chipmunk

itself. This diurnal rodent mainly forages on the ground but sometimes in trees, and stores are stockpiled for winter. Mating generally takes place in April and May; 28 to 30 days later, four to eight babies are born naked, eyes closed, in an underground burrow or cliff den. Cliff chipmunks appear protective of their home area and may chase intruders away. They also are quite vocal, emitting various barks and chirps.
SIMILAR SPECIES: The gray-collared chipmunk (parts of Mogollon Rim) has distinct light and dark dorsal stripes. Several other chipmunk species inhabit small areas near Arizona's borders.

Cliff chipmunk

Gunnison's prairie dogs

GUNNISON'S PRAIRIE DOG
Cynomys gunnisoni

DESCRIPTION: Golden tan tinged with black above; buff below; tiny ears; short, thin tail with white tip; sometimes confused with round-tailed ground squirrel, but much larger
SIZE: Length of 10 to 12 inches, plus tail of about 2 inches; weight of 1.5 to 2.5 pounds
DIET: Grasses, seeds and shoots
HABITAT: Grasslands and montane valleys from 6,000 to 12,000 feet
DISTRIBUTION: Northeastern, East-Central and parts of Central Arizona
■ These colonial rodents live in "towns." Winters are spent underground, but from March to

October, the prairie dogs are up and about. When spring-born pups (one to eight per litter) begin romping around in early summer, adults increase their sentry duties. They take turns perching atop the dirt mounds that mark entrances to their subterranean labyrinths. Prairie-dog vocalizations have been researched at length, and the results suggest their language includes at least 100 words, including nouns and modifiers. Different alarm barks communicate specific details about potential predators, such as species, speed and direction of travel, and even color. Some of the language, once learned, may even be decipherable to the human ear. Prairie dogs are ecologically valuable. Like gophers, they aerate the earth, encourage plant growth and create protective habitat for other animals. Plus, they are intrinsically linked with

RANDALL D. BABB, ARIZONA GAME AND FISH DEPARTMENT

SIZE: Length of 6 to 7 inches, plus tail of 2.5 to 3 inches; weight of 3 to 8 ounces; male larger than female
DIET: Roots, bulbs, tubers and some other plant matter
HABITAT: Desert scrub, grasslands, woodland meadows, fields and agricultural areas below timberline; prefers open areas with soft soil
DISTRIBUTION: Statewide

■ Solitary and almost always underground, a gopher can be challenging to spot. But its handiwork is not. Fan-shaped dirt mounds from digging extensive subterranean tunnel systems (up to 150 feet long) mark the land wherever it resides. Sizable internal chambers are padded with grass for daytime sleeping or designated for food or waste storage. This animal approaches vegetation from underneath — it burrows to the roots and pulls down the edible parts. The "pocket" in its name refers to deep, fur-lined cheek pouches that are used to carry stores. Breeding is ordinarily in springtime, and gestation is a mere 18 or 19 days. Most gophers produce just one litter a year, but Arizona Botta's may have multiple broods, each averaging six pups. With predators such as badgers, foxes, coyotes and owls, most gophers survive about 2.5 years. Although considered pests in certain agricultural areas, these rodents are actually good for soil health.

endangered black-footed ferrets. Unfortunately, millions have been exterminated by humans or lost to plague. Efforts are now underway to preserve remaining populations.
SIMILAR SPECIES: The black-tailed prairie dog, historically found in the southeastern corner of Arizona, was extirpated by 1960. Reintroductions began in 2008 with the goal of re-establishing that species in Arizona.

BOTTA'S POCKET GOPHER
Thomomys bottae

DESCRIPTION: Coppery brown with gray flecking; white spotting on chin; small dark patch behind each tiny ear; mostly hairless tail; prominent yellow-orange incisors; long front claws

Botta's pocket gopher

ORD'S KANGAROO RAT
Dipodomys ordii

DESCRIPTION: Looks somewhat like a gerbil; tawny with dark flecks above, white below; white spot over each large eye and behind each small, round ear; extremely long, striped tail has dark, tufted tip; sits up on long (2 inches) hind feet
SIZE: Length of 3.5 to 4 inches, plus tail of 4.5 to 6.5 inches
DIET: Mostly seeds; some other plant matter
HABITAT: Desert scrub, grasslands, woodlands and forests
DISTRIBUTION: Northern, Central and Southeastern Arizona

■ Here is a charismatic rodent noted for its distinctive shape and locomotion. The kangaroo rat, which normally hops or ambles on all fours, is sometimes glimpsed scurrying through a beam of headlights. But when necessary, this tiny dynamo can leap an impressive 8 feet. Its tiny hind legs are adept at grasping and plucking seeds during its nocturnal foraging, and fur-lined cheek pouches transport harvested food back to its home. Burrow entrances, about 3 inches across and usually on a slope, are closed during the day with dirt and debris. Solitary by nature, kangaroo rats interact only for mating. This species reproduces year-round, in sync with seasonal plant growth, and each litter averages three to five pups. Adapted to Arizona's arid climate, the kangaroo rat drinks little or no water and cleans its fur with dust baths.

SIMILAR SPECIES: Other species in Arizona are the Merriam's kangaroo rat (west, south and east-central), desert kangaroo rat (far west and most of southwest), banner-tailed kangaroo rat (southeast) and chisel-toothed kangaroo rat (extreme northwest).

WHITE-THROATED WOODRAT or PACKRAT
Neotoma albigula

DESCRIPTION: Mouse-like shape; grayish tan above; white throat; furry tail; large, rounded ears; dark, bulbous eyes; long whiskers
SIZE: Length of 7 to 9.5 inches, plus tail of 5 to 7 inches; weight of 5 to 10 ounces; male larger than female
DIET: Mostly cactuses (especially prickly pear); some other plant matter, seeds and fruits
HABITAT: Desert scrub, grasslands, arid

Ord's kangaroo rat

White-throated woodrat

woodlands, forests and urban areas
DISTRIBUTION: Statewide, except extreme northwest corner

■ A packrat's nights are spent collecting — bones, twigs, scat, feathers — with a special affection for shiny things, like earrings found in or around human dwellings. These rodents are famous for caching objects at their nest, referred to as a midden (an archaeological term meaning "garbage pile"). Only one adult at a time uses the internal den, but over generations, several take residence; each enlarges the heap. An average midden, piled with sticks and protective cactus spines, reaches 8 feet long and 3 feet tall. Paleoecologists study fossilized midden content, some of which dates back more than 40,000 years, providing insight into the flora and fauna of ancient Arizona. Packrats can climb well and scamper fast and are always on the lookout for predators. Males mark territory using scent glands located on their bellies. Like Ord's kangaroo rats, packrats drum their hind feet for communication and during courtship. Breeding occurs from January to August and results in multiple litters.

LIVING WITH WILDLIFE

Now and then, packrats construct nests in human spaces — houses, yards, even cars — and their middens can cause quite a mess. The best way to keep them out is to maintain a closed-door policy. Fill cracks along fences and walls, place screening over water-shed holes and keep defunct vehicles garaged. If a packrat does become a disturbance, a live trap can be rented to capture and relocate. If relocation is not an option, a "snap trap" is the only humane alternative. Never use poisons or glue boards, which can indiscriminately kill other wildlife.

Offspring (usually two or three) are born after 30 to 38 days of pregnancy. They reach maturity and establish their own dens by about six months of age.

SIMILAR SPECIES: All woodrats are known as packrats; there are five other species in Arizona, but given their limited ranges, they are less frequently seen.

DESERT COTTONTAIL
Sylvilagus audubonii

DESCRIPTION: Roundish body; tan peppered gray above, white below (including tail that folds up); rusty nape and legs; long, erect ears; dark eyes
SIZE: Length of 12 to 14 inches, plus tail of 1 to 2 inches; weight of 1.5 to 2.5 pounds; much smaller than a jackrabbit
DIET: Herbivorous; grasses, forbs, shrubs and some acorns
HABITAT: Desert scrub, grasslands, woodlands, agricultural areas and urban areas; below 7,500 feet
DISTRIBUTION: Nearly statewide

▪ These crepuscular rabbits are commonplace in all but the most developed environments. They are quick to hide under vegetation, and whenever watchful, the white of the tail is flashed (much like Coues deer). Cautious movements belie their ability to sprint up to 15 mph and swim if necessary. Many rabbit species dig burrow systems, but not cottontails. They don't even give birth underground. A simple depression lined with weeds and the mother's fur acts as a natal nest. Young, born naked with eyes closed, must rely on stillness and camouflage for protection. Breeding is practically year-round, and females, who reach maturity after only three months, average five litters per year with two to four kits each. Prolific reproduction is necessary because most will not survive the year.

SIMILAR SPECIES: The Eastern cottontail (parts of northwest, central and southeast) and mountain cottontail (parts of north and east-central, above 7,500 feet) may be difficult to distinguish.

BLACK-TAILED JACKRABBIT
Lepus californicus

DESCRIPTION: Lean, angular frame; grizzled gray-brown with black stripe on tail; white below; enormous (up to 6 inches) black-tipped ears; amber eyes
SIZE: Length of 18 to 21 inches, plus head of 3 to 4 inches; weight of 4 to 7.5 pounds
DIET: Grasses, forbs, shrubs, cactus and their own soft droppings (to extract moisture and nutrients)
HABITAT: Desert scrub, grasslands, open woodlands and agricultural areas
DISTRIBUTION: Statewide

▪ Jackrabbits are hares. While rabbits and hares are both leporids (family *Leporidae*) and share a lot of characteristics, there is one profound difference. Unlike rabbits, hare babies, called leverets, are precocial, meaning they're born well-furred, with eyes open, and are mobile within an hour. Jackrabbits mainly breed from December to July, and dramatic courtship behaviors between bucks and does include competitive leaps and chases. Pregnancy lasts 41 to 47 days, and a mother usually delivers two leverets per brood. She leaves them alone, returning to nurse every evening for three to four weeks until they are weaned. She will raise several litters per season. Foraging is done at night, and days are passed dozing in the bushes. Oversized ears not only bestow exceptional hearing but also help control body temperature; the hare can perk them to dissipate summer heat or flatten them into winter blankets. All leporids are built for evasive running, but jackrabbits have exceedingly long limbs and can

Desert cottontail

Black-tailed jackrabbit

spring up to 20 feet. Quickly accelerating to 35 mph, the jack darts in wild zigzags, making it nearly impossible to follow. It thumps its feet to warn others of danger.

SIMILAR SPECIES: The antelope jackrabbit (parts of Southern Arizona) is larger and has longer ears and whitish flanks. The antlered "jackalope" is mythical and does not exist.

LIVING WITH WILDLIFE

If a jackrabbit or cottontail baby (or deer fawn) is found alone, do not move or disturb it unless there is immediate danger. Mothers purposely leave them unattended and only occasionally return for nursing.

Cooper's hawk

BIRDS

BIRDS OF PREY

The Latin origin of raptor is *rapere*. It means "to take by force." Raptors are hunters — recognized for their binocular vision and robust legs ending in powerful claws, called talons, which are designed to grasp and kill small animals like the teeth of a lion. These specialized birds of prey swallow their catch whole or consume chunks ripped off with hooked bills. Unable to digest the solid parts, they cast pellets — regurgitated balls of bones, fur and feathers. Like other birds, they are built for flight: lightweight, with beaks instead of teeth and honeycombed bones. There are 42 raptor species in Arizona, currently divided into two taxonomic orders: *Falconiformes* and *Strigiformes*. *Falconiformes* (diurnal raptors) includes eagles, hawks and falcons. Carrion-eating vultures and condors are also currently in this order, although some ornithologists advocate reclassifying them into their own order, *Cathartiformes*. Lacking grasping talons, they do not actually kill any prey; instead, they scavenge carcasses with meat-tearing bills. Owls make up the order *Strigiformes* (nocturnal raptors) and have traits particular to life in the dark. Owls have soft-edged primary feathers that are quiet against the night air. Hearing is bolstered by larger eardrums and prominent facial discs, smoothly concaved feathers around the eyes that collect sound waves and direct them to the ears. Night vision is enhanced by extra-large eyeballs — so large, in fact, there is no room for musculature to roll them. To compensate, an owl's neck rotates 270 degrees. Most raptors exhibit size-based sexual dimorphism, with females up to 50 percent heavier than their male counterparts, depending on species. (In non-raptors, males are more likely to be larger.) Nesting typically begins in spring. As with all birds, the male mounts the female for mating and tails are adjusted until cloacas touch. Offspring tend to be drab in coloring, and some take years to develop adult plumage. When summer temperatures soar, raptors may be seen cooling off with an open-mouth throat vibration called gular fluttering.

Bald eagle

Bald eagle

BALD EAGLE

Haliaeetus leucocephalus

DESCRIPTION: Chocolate brown overall, white head and tail, yellow bill and legs; wing position in flight is flat and level; all-brown yearling may appear similar to golden eagle, but lacks golden nape and has larger head

SIZE: Length of 28 to 37 inches; wingspan of 5.5 to 7.5 feet; weight of 6 to 9.5 pounds; female larger than male

DIET: Opportunistic carnivore; fish, carrion, mammals and water birds; sometimes steals from other raptors

HABITAT: Forests, riparian woodlands, wetlands and canyons

DISTRIBUTION: Statewide; year-round in central river zones, winter everywhere else

NEST AND EGGS: Near water (often Salt and Verde rivers); 5- to 6-foot stick platform in trees, cliffs or pinnacles; one to three eggs, incubation 34 to 36 days

CONSERVATION STATUS: Removed from endangered-species list in 2007, but still federally protected under the Bald and Golden Eagle Protection Act

■ Eagles often mate for life, and the aerial courtship of these enormous birds is quite spectacular — grasping talons in midair and plummeting hundreds of feet. Nesting takes place in the same area each year, earlier than other raptors, with eggs laid by January or February. Fledglings take their first flight within three months of hatching but must wait five years to fully develop adult plumage. They may live more than 25 years in the wild. In 1782, the bald eagle was chosen as America's national bird. When it was listed as endangered in 1973, people rallied to protect it by banning DDT, an insecticide that damaged egg production in many avian species. Thankfully, recovery was successful and bald eagles are still seen soaring across Arizona skies.

GOLDEN EAGLE
Aquila chrysaetos

DESCRIPTION: Brown overall, coppery highlights on nape of neck, faint banding on tail; unlike bald eagle, wings may be slightly angled up when soaring
SIZE: Length of 27 to 33 inches; wingspan of 6 to 7.5 feet; weight of 6.5 to 13.5 pounds; female larger than male
DIET: Mostly mid-sized mammals (especially jackrabbits and prairie dogs)

HABITAT: Desert scrub, grasslands, sparse woodlands, forests and canyons
DISTRIBUTION: Statewide
NEST AND EGGS: Both sexes collect materials for 5– to 6-foot cupped platform, usually on a cliff but sometimes in a tree; one to three eggs, incubation 41 to 45 days

■ Like bald eagles, the golden eagle performs amazing aerobatics. "Sky dancing" is a series of steep, rapid dives transitioning to powerful upward swoops — sometimes the eagle retraces its path back and forth, like a skateboarder in a practice bowl. It may even play with objects in flight. Its hunting strategy is to circle above the ground, then rapidly angle toward its prey before making a quick dive to capture it. Although the female does most of the incubating, her mate may occasionally help. Eaglets are able to tear delivered meat and self-feed in about one and a half months and leave the nest in three months. The golden eagle is protected by the federal Bald and Golden Eagle Protection Act. Normally quiet, it may occasionally make a small *culp* sound.

Golden eagle

HARRIS' HAWK

Parabuteo unicinctus

DESCRIPTION: Dark brown overall, rufous shoulders and thighs, white at tail's base and tip; yellow legs and feet

SIZE: Length of 18 to 23 inches; wingspan of 3.5 to 4 feet; weight of 1 to 3.5 pounds; female larger than male

DIET: Rabbits, rodents, reptiles, birds and large insects

HABITAT: Desert scrub, mesquite woods, grasslands, canyons, riparian areas and urban areas

DISTRIBUTION: Much of Southern Arizona

NEST AND EGGS: Cupped stick platform, often in mesquite tree or saguaro; usually three or four eggs, incubation 33 to 36 days; up to three broods

■ Harris' hawks are exceptional in that they hunt in groups, like wolves, with one flushing out prey for the others to capture. Social units (three to seven birds) often include adult offspring, which may remain with their parents for up to three years and help raise younger siblings. Breeding triads — one male and two females, or two males and one female — occasionally form and produce offspring. And now and then, these birds exhibit an even more peculiar behavior called stacking, where each one sits atop the next. Naturally vocal, this species commonly emits a scratchy, descending *arrrr*. It perches with a more horizontal posture than the upright red-tailed hawk.

SIMILAR SPECIES: The common black hawk (northwest, along Mogollon Rim to southeast) is sooty black overall with a white mid-tail bar.

Harris' hawk

Western red-tailed hawk

WESTERN RED-TAILED HAWK
Buteo jamaicensis calurus

DESCRIPTION: Coloration can vary, but usually warm brown above and streaked buffy below; tail cinnamon above and pale tan-orange below; dark bar at leading edge of wing visible in flight

SIZE: Length of 17 to 22 inches; wingspan of 3.5 to 4.5 feet; weight of 1.75 to 2.5 pounds; female larger than male

DIET: Mostly small mammals; some reptiles and birds

HABITAT: Every habitat across Arizona, including urban areas

DISTRIBUTION: Statewide

NEST AND EGGS: Both sexes build or refurbish bulky stick bowl, usually in a tree or on a cliff ledge, but sometimes in a saguaro; two or three eggs, incubation 28 to 35 days

■ The red-tailed hawk is the most commonly seen hawk in Arizona. Soaring the skies on broad, rounded wings, its tail flashes umber whenever it tips to the side. Like the Harris' hawk, this species regularly perches atop roadside posts where it is easily noticed. Its harsh call — a descending *quee-rrr* — has become symbolic of all hawks. A male red-tailed puts on aerial displays during courtship and helps his mate care for offspring. Fledglings exit the nest after six to seven weeks but cannot fly well for at least two weeks longer. These hawks attack in a slow, controlled dive.

Cooper's hawk

COOPER'S HAWK
Accipiter cooperii

DESCRIPTION: Slate gray above and barred rufous below; dark cap and reddish eyes; long tail with dark bands and rounded trailing edge
SIZE: Length of 14 to 18 inches; wingspan of 2 to 3 feet; weight of up to 1 pound; female larger than male
DIET: Mostly birds; some small mammals and lizards
HABITAT: Woodlands, forests and urban areas
DISTRIBUTION: Statewide; migrates away from the hottest southwestern deserts during summer
NEST AND EGGS: Cupped stick pile, usually in a tree; three to five eggs, incubation 34 to 36 days

■ This crow-sized bird has short, rounded wings and a long, narrow tail for excellent aerial maneuverability — it flies with a quick rhythm of "flap, flap, flap ... glide." Hatchling Cooper's hawks have gray-green eyes, which turn bright yellow in juveniles before transitioning to the deep red of adulthood. The male does most of the hunting for his family through the nesting period (four to five weeks).
SIMILAR SPECIES: The sharp-shinned hawk (similar range) has near-identical plumage but is smaller (about 12 inches) with a slightly shorter, squared-off tail.

AMERICAN KESTREL
Falco sparverius

DESCRIPTION: Rusty red back, gray-blue wings, cinnamon tail with black bar near tip; female is ruddy brown above, pale-streaked underparts and several dark, muted bars on tail; both sexes have gray crown and two dark, vertical cheek stripes
SIZE: America's smallest falcon, with length of 8.5 to 12 inches; wingspan of up to 2 feet; weight of 3 to 6 ounces; female larger than male
DIET: Mostly invertebrates (especially

American kestrel

grasshoppers); some birds, lizards and rodents

HABITAT: Desert scrub, grasslands, woodlands, forests, agricultural land and urban areas

DISTRIBUTION: Statewide

NEST AND EGGS: Cavity (woodpecker hole or nest box); four or five eggs, incubation 29 to 31 days

■ This is one of only a few raptors that show sexual dimorphism in coloring as well as size. Bird counts suggest kestrels are declining in Arizona, yet they are still widespread and fairly prevalent — often seen perched upon fence posts and telephone wires, bobbing their tails. Their call is a rapid *killy-killy-killy!* In flight, wings are distinctly pointed, and these agile predators have the ability to hover, briefly holding position before diving down to seize prey. They have been reported to cache food, sometimes out in the open.

AMERICAN PEREGRINE FALCON
Falco peregrinus anatum

DESCRIPTION: Dark gray above, buffy underparts with barred belly and thighs; black helmet extends down in sideburns; long, pointed wings appear swept back in flight
SIZE: Length of 14 to 19 inches; wingspan of about 3.5 feet; female larger than male
DIET: Primarily birds (caught in flight); some bats; occasionally steals from other raptors
HABITAT: Desert scrub, grasslands, canyons, wetlands and urban areas; especially near cliffs
DISTRIBUTION: Statewide; year-round in moderate elevations, summer in highest mountains and winter in lowest deserts
NEST AND EGGS: Scraped depression on high cliff, bridge or building ledge; three or four eggs, incubation 33 to 35 days
CONSERVATION STATUS: Removed from endangered-species list in 1999

■ Here is the world's fastest animal. A peregrine can fly level at nearly 70 mph and — wings tucked for a dive — has been clocked at speeds over 230 mph. With such aerobatic prowess, it is a proficient hunter. Peregrine means "wandering," and many do seasonally migrate around the state. Mating pairs appear monogamous. The male may help incubate eggs, and both parents deliver food to their nestlings, which fledge in about one and a half months. The peregrine falcon once was endangered: In the mid-20th century, its eggs suffered thinning effects from the insecticide DDT, causing populations to fall into rapid decline. As with bald eagles, the species took decades to recover.

American peregrine falcon

TURKEY VULTURE

Cathartes aura

DESCRIPTION: Brownish black overall; small, featherless red head and white-tipped bill; silvery underside of primary feathers gives two-toned appearance in flight; wings held in a distinctive "V" shape (dihedral) when soaring
SIZE: Length of 25 to 32 inches; wingspan of up to 6 feet; weight of 2 to 4 pounds; no obvious sexual dimorphism
DIET: Carrion (prefers fresh vertebrate meat)
HABITAT: Desert scrub, broken forests, agricultural land and urban areas (especially roadsides and dumps); prefers open areas
DISTRIBUTION: Statewide in summer, southern regions in winter
NEST AND EGGS: Depression in hollow (cave, cliff, tree or log); two eggs, incubation 38 to 41 days

■ Most birds have a poorly developed sense of smell, but not turkey vultures — with wide nasal openings, these scavengers can sniff rotting flesh 50 miles away. Vultures are social feeders, and several may gather at one carcass; naked heads help the birds stay clean when poking them in the muck. Because of their gorging habits, turkey vultures can survive two weeks without food. Cold mornings are spent perched, black wings open to the sun. In the hottest months, urine is dribbled down scaly legs to create evaporative cooling, called urohydrosis. These same thermal-regulating behaviors are used by condors. Parents share incubation duties, and chicks, fed by regurgitation, fledge in nine to 10 weeks. Regurgitation is also used to drive away potential predators, which are repelled by the stench. For all their distasteful characteristics, turkey vultures play a critical role in environmental cleanup. And they are quite beautiful to behold in flight. A kettle of them may soar together for hours without flapping, wheeling on warm upward currents of air called thermals. Their teetering dihedrals are easily recognized, even at a distance.
SIMILAR SPECIES: The black vulture (from Phoenix into southeast) has a dark-gray head and a shorter tail, and the whitish undersides of its wingtips are visible in flight.

Turkey vultures

California condor

CALIFORNIA CONDOR

Gymnogyps californianus

DESCRIPTION: Black overall; naked, salmon-colored head and reddish eyes; fleshy patch of chest skin visible with full crop; white patches on underwings visible in flight; in cold weather, cowl of downy neck feathers raises like a hood

SIZE: Largest flying land bird in North America, with length of 46 to 53 inches; wingspan of up to 9.5 feet; weight of 17 to 26 pounds; no obvious sexual dimorphism

DIET: Carrion (especially large mammals)

HABITAT: Canyons and forests

DISTRIBUTION: Grand Canyon region

NEST AND EGGS: Cliffside cave or ledge, only accessible by flight; one egg, incubation 54 to 58 days

CONSERVATION STATUS: Endangered

■ Condors are highly social birds that roost and dine in groups, using body language, grunts and hisses to communicate. They typically mate for life (which may be more than 60 years), and parenting is handled as a team. A condor chick remains in the nest longer than most birds: six months. It will not reach adulthood for six to eight years. This scavenger spends much of its time airborne, gliding along the cliffs, wings flat as an airplane. With a poor sense of smell, it employs sight — like a conflux of vultures — to locate carrion. Ten thousand years ago, wide-ranging condors fed on megafauna such as mammoths and mastodons. Populations plummeted by the 1800s, and by 1981, there were only 22 left on the planet. Through intensive captive breeding and reintroduction, condors are making an against-all-odds comeback. Today, lead poisoning is the gravest threat to the survival of the species — dozens have died from eating meat tainted with lead shot. Hunters who use lead-free ammunition are helping to create a better future for this magnificent bird.

HOW TO IDENTIFY RAPTORS IN FLIGHT

Bald eagle

Golden eagle

Harris' hawk

Cooper's hawk

American kestrel

American peregrine falcon

Turkey vulture

California condor

Western red-tailed hawk

Barn owl

BARN OWL
Tyto alba

DESCRIPTION: Pale cinnamon with gray smudging above, white with black flecking below; white, heart-shaped facial disc; dark eyes; females tend to have slightly darker plumage

SIZE: Length of 12.5 to 16 inches; wingspan of 3 to 4 feet; female larger than male

DIET: Mostly rodents

HABITAT: Grasslands, desert scrub, riparian areas, agricultural land and urban areas; below 4,200 feet

DISTRIBUTION: Statewide; summer in northeast quarter, year-round everywhere else

NEST AND EGGS: Cavity (tree, building, cliff or nest box); four to six eggs, incubation 29 to 34 days; up to three broods

■ Even when residing close to humans, barn owls are infrequently seen as they cast their white shadows across the night sky. Some owls, including this species, have asymmetrical ear holes. One is higher and points slightly downward, and the other is lower and points slightly upward. By triangulating sound, the owl can capture prey — like a mouse under leaves — using no vision whatsoever. Barn owls hunt over open fields with slow, buoyant wing beats. They do not hoot like other owls. Instead, they make a variety of raspy screeches, *kleak-kleak* calls and hissing sounds.

LIVING WITH WILDLIFE
In their normal life cycle, many baby birds depart the nest before they can really fly and spend several days on the ground, fed by their parent(s). Humans who encounter fledglings at this stage may mistakenly assume they are orphaned, but it is best not to interfere unless the youngster is injured or no parent arrives after extensive monitoring. An immature chick can be returned to its nest without concern of rejection, since birds generally have a poor sense of smell. For assistance with wildlife concerns, see page 152.

Great horned owls
(adult and nestlings)

GREAT HORNED OWL
Bubo virginianus

DESCRIPTION: Bulky brown shape, mottled or barred with white; lighter underparts; pale-ochre facial discs; white throat line; prominent "ear" tufts; yellow eyes
SIZE: Length of 18 to 25 inches; wingspan of 3.5 to 4.5 feet; weight of 2 to 5.5 pounds; female larger than male
DIET: Opportunistic carnivore; mammals, birds (including other raptors), reptiles and invertebrates
HABITAT: Almost all Arizona habitats, including urban areas

DISTRIBUTION: Statewide
NEST AND EGGS: Uses old nest from another bird in tree or cavity, occasionally on ground; two or three eggs, incubation 28 to 35 days
■ The long feather tufts on a great horned owl's head are not ears, but decorative plumage. This raptor's enormous talons can exert tremendous pressure, giving it the power to attack animals larger than itself. Mates stick together, although the female does the majority of parental work. This nocturnal raptor's low *hoo, hoo-hoo* has become the iconic sound of a rural night.
SIMILAR SPECIES: The long-eared owl (almost statewide) is smaller (about 15 inches) and distinctly slender, with ear tufts that point straight up.

BURROWING OWL
Athene cunicularia

DESCRIPTION: Umber brown with white spots above, tan-white with brown barring below; broad, rounded head; yellow eyes under white brow; short tail; distinctly long legs

SIZE: Length of 7.5 to 10 inches; wingspan of 21 to 24 inches; weight of 4 to 8 ounces; males are larger in size, but females often are heavier

DIET: Invertebrates and rodents

HABITAT: Desert scrub, grasslands, agricultural land and urban areas (especially fields and golf courses)

DISTRIBUTION: Statewide; year-round toward south and west, summer everywhere else

NEST AND EGGS: Often small colonies; dirt burrow or hole in tree or building; seven to 10 eggs, incubation 28 to 30 days

■ This ground-dwelling raptor lives in abandoned mammal burrows and is most frequently seen standing outside its hole like a sentinel — or perched atop a dirt mound, rock or low fence post. A crepuscular hunter, it may hop after scurrying prey or drop down from a perch. Flight is typically low, with jerky wing beats. A burrowing owl exhibits enchanting behaviors: It may turn its head upside down when curious, and when threatened, it pops up and down like a bobblehead. Although this species has at least 17 vocalizations, the primary song is a two-note *coo-coo*. Owlets also produce an alarm call that imitates the *buzz* of a rattlesnake. The father delivers food while the mother tends their young. By lining her brooding nest with dung (especially cow dung), she may attract dung beetles, a favored food.

Burrowing owl

WOODPECKERS

The family *Picidae* unites the wood-pecking birds. Some are actually called woodpeckers, while others go by different names, such as flickers and sapsuckers. These zygodactyl birds possess short legs with strong claws for clinging to vertical surfaces, and most lean on stiff tail feathers for stabilization. A strong, pointed bill is used to chisel holes; then, a barbed tongue, which can be twice the length of the bill, penetrates those holes to extract food — namely insects. Other foodstuffs supplement their diet. Woodpeckers also bore nesting and roosting cavities, which provide shelter for many other animals. And they are notorious for drumming on hard, resonating surfaces, tapping rapid territorial communications like some kind of avian Morse code. Breeding season ranges from March to July. Most species are sexually dimorphic, and monogamous pairs share parenting responsibilities, although the male often excavates the nest and/or takes the night shift for incubation and chick care. Fledglings depart the nest by one month of age.

ACORN WOODPECKER
Melanerpes formicivorus

DESCRIPTION: Black above; black-and-white streaks on chest; white belly and rump; pale-yellow forehead and chin; white eyes; white wing patches visible in flight; both sexes have red cap (larger on male)
SIZE: Length of about 9 inches; wingspan of 14 to 17 inches

Acorn woodpecker (female)

DIET: Mostly insects and acorns; some sap, fruits, seeds, nuts and bird eggs
HABITAT: Oak and pine-oak woodlands, from 3,800 to 8,500 feet
DISTRIBUTION: Northern and Eastern Arizona
NEST AND EGGS: Bores cavity in large tree, usually in dead wood; three to six eggs, incubation 11 to 14 days; one to three broods
■ A group of acorn woodpeckers is called a bushel — and a bushel of these birds is fascinating. Working together in a complex social colony (up to 16 individuals), they harvest fall acorns and stuff them into small, chiseled holes in what is referred to as a granary tree. Used over generations and potentially riddled with some 50,000 holes, the granary tree is always under guard. Acorn woodpeckers rarely drill for insects, preferring to catch flying ants, bees and beetles right out of the air. As cooperative nesters, several helpers may provide incubation and chick care for a single nest. *Wake-up wake-up!* is their exclamatory call.

GILA WOODPECKER
Melanerpes uropygialis

DESCRIPTION: Pale sandy gray with zebra barring on upper parts; white wing patches visible in flight; male has red cap
SIZE: Length of 8 to 10 inches; wingspan of 15 to 18 inches
DIET: Insects, fruits, seeds and nectar; occasionally small vertebrates and bird eggs

Gila woodpecker (male)

HABITAT: Desert scrub, riparian corridors and urban areas, up to 4,800 feet
DISTRIBUTION: Southern and West-Central Arizona
NEST AND EGGS: Bores cavity, usually in saguaro but sometimes in riparian tree; three to five eggs, incubation 13 to 14 days; two or three broods

■ The Gila woodpecker is a keystone desert species — not only because its cavities are used by an array of animals, but also because it plays a role in cactus pollination and seed dispersal (like the lesser long-nosed bat). Nesting holes are drilled months in advance, allowing time for the saguaro's inner pulp to become suitably dry. This woodpecker is especially antagonistic toward other birds. Its call is a series of sharp *pip* notes or a rolling *churrrr*.
SIMILAR SPECIES: The ladder-backed woodpecker (similar range) has black stripes on its face.

Northern flicker (male)

NORTHERN FLICKER
Colaptes auratus

DESCRIPTION: Brown with black bars above, tan with black spots below; white rump; black bib; gray cheeks and throat; reddish wing linings are visible in flight; male has red mustache
SIZE: Length of 12 to 14 inches; wingspan of 17 to 21 inches
DIET: Mostly ants; some other insects and fruits; occasional seeds and nuts
HABITAT: Open woodlands and broken forests, desert scrub, agricultural areas and urban parks; more common at lower elevations in winter
DISTRIBUTION: Statewide; winter in southwest, year-round everywhere else
NEST AND EGGS: Bores cavity in tree, usually dead or diseased wood; five to eight eggs, incubation 11 to 16 days; one or two broods
■ This is Arizona's most widely distributed woodpecker. Unlike its cousins, the northern flicker often forages on the ground, drilling the dirt for ants. And it is more likely to perch on a horizontal branch than hitch itself to a tree trunk. In flight, however, it is a typical woodpecker — rising and dipping as it flaps and glides.
SIMILAR SPECIES: The gilded flicker (southwest) is slightly smaller and has yellow wing linings.

RED-NAPED SAPSUCKER
Sphyrapicus nuchalis

DESCRIPTION: Black-and-white checkered above, pale yellow-tan with gray speckles below; distinctive white stripe on wing; head has bold black-and-white stripes, with red forehead, nape and throat; female has white chin
SIZE: Length of 8 to 9 inches; wingspan of 16 to 18 inches
DIET: Mostly insects and sap; occasional fruits and berries
HABITAT: Forests, woodlands and riparian areas
DISTRIBUTION: Higher elevations in Northeastern Arizona in summer; southern half of the state in winter
NEST AND EGGS: Bores cavity in aspen tree; four to six eggs, incubation 12 to 13 days
■ It's easy to tell if there are sapsuckers around, because tree trunks are marked with small, squarish pits in neat, horizontal rows. The drillers frequently return to these sites to lap the emerging sap and eat insects attracted by the ooze. Other birds, including hummingbirds, also feed at sap wells. The principal call of the red-naped sapsucker is a mewing *mee-ah.*

Red-naped sapsucker (male)

Lesser nighthawk

LESSER NIGHTHAWK
Chordeiles acutipennis

DESCRIPTION: Mottled dusty brown above, barred gray and buff below; short legs; tiny bill; white throat; large, dark eyes; long tail is slightly notched; wings long, pointed and angled back, with conspicuous white bar near wingtip visible in flight; in female, tan throat and wing bars

SIZE: Length of 8 to 9 inches; wingspan of 21 inches

DIET: Flying insects

HABITAT: Desert scrub, grasslands, agricultural land and urban areas; prefers nearby water

DISTRIBUTION: Western, Central and Southern Arizona

NEST AND EGGS: Scrape on ground or occasionally flat rooftop; two eggs, incubation 18 to 19 days

■ The nighthawk hunts on the wing but is not a bird of prey — lacking talons, it captures food in its gaping mouth. After migrating to Mexico for winter, this species arrives back in Arizona as early as March and stays until October. On summer evenings, they can be seen erratically fluttering and diving around streetlights, foraging on insects attracted to the light. They also mix with bats over grassy parks. Nighthawks spend their days sleeping and have such effective camouflage they are rarely spotted amid the native vegetation. Males can sometimes be heard softly trilling. The female handles incubation, but both sexes feed the chicks.

SIMILAR SPECIES: The common nighthawk (north and east in summer) is slightly larger and darker, with a white bar farther from the wingtip.

MOURNING DOVE
Zenaida macroura

DESCRIPTION: Grayish tan above, lighter below; black spots on upper wing; single dark spot under eye; in flight, tail shaped like long, pointed dart; male has pink-purple hues on chest and neck

SIZE: Length of 11 to 14 inches; wingspan of 17 to 19 inches

DIET: Seeds

HABITAT: All habitats below 9,000 feet, except the most heavily forested areas

DISTRIBUTION: Statewide

NEST AND EGGS: Loose platform of twigs, usually elevated; two eggs, incubation 13 to 15 days; two or three broods

■ These seed eaters forage on the ground, then perch higher up to digest. Swift in flight, their wings make a characteristic whistle on take-off. Mourning doves were named for their plaintive (and owl-like) *co-OO-oo-oo-oo* — a call that denotes the onset of spring. Soon, mating pairs are found incubating eggs. Since the father takes the day shift, he is more likely to be seen atop the nest. Chicks — which are fed crop milk, a nutritious liquid produced by both parents — are fully independent by a month of age.

SIMILAR SPECIES: The Inca dove (central and south) is significantly smaller (about 8 inches), and its overall plumage appears scaled, with rufous wingtips.

WHITE-WINGED DOVE
Zenaida asiatica

DESCRIPTION: Gray-brown above, lighter below; distinctive white patch on upper wing; reddish eye with blue skin and dark line below; white-tipped tail fanned in flight (not wedged, like mourning dove)

SIZE: Length of 11 to 12 inches; wingspan of 17 to 18 inches

DIET: Saguaro nectar, pollen, fruits and seeds

HABITAT: Desert scrub, riparian corridors and urban areas

Mourning doves (female, left, and male)

White-winged dove

DISTRIBUTION: Southern and West-Central Arizona in summer; parts of southeast year-round
NEST AND EGGS: Sometimes loose colonies; flimsy twig platform in tree, shrub or cactus; two eggs, incubation 13 to 14 days; two or three broods

■ In the Sonoran Desert, the white-winged dove has an ecological dependence on saguaro cactuses — heavily relying on them for food, plus serving as an important pollinator and seed disperser. As with the mourning dove, the male gathers materials while the female constructs their nest. Infant care is also similar, and both species will feign a broken wing to lure predators away. Doves have a rare ability among birds: They can swallow water without lifting their heads.

MERRIAM'S TURKEY
Meleagris gallopavo merriami

DESCRIPTION: Dark, iridescent green-bronze overall; black chest tuft; thin, white bars on wings; cream-tipped rump and tail feathers; bare head pink to blue, with red wattles; male has spurred legs and fans tail feathers for display; female more dull
SIZE: Length of 3 to 4 feet; wingspan of 4 to 5 feet; weight of 8 to 24 pounds; male larger than female

DIET: Invertebrates, acorns (a favorite), seeds, grasses and berries
HABITAT: Forest, woodlands and grasslands; 3,500 to 10,000 feet
DISTRIBUTION: Scattered along diagonal from Northwestern to Central Arizona
NEST AND EGGS: Shallow depression hidden on ground; 10 to 12 eggs (on average), incubation about 28 days

■ Wild turkeys are watchful, intelligent birds. By day, they scratch the ground for edibles. By night, they take to the trees to roost. During breeding season (March to June), excited toms strut about, feathers puffed, and their noisy gobbling can be heard a mile away. Large harems form for mating, after which hens move into dense habitat to lay eggs. Mother Merriam's raise their precocial chicks alone, and the brood will stay with her until winter, when they gather into flocks along the snow line. Predators — including humans, coyotes, raccoons, hawks, snakes and even ground squirrels — are a constant threat. But wild turkeys are fast runners. And they're surprisingly good fliers, able to quickly flush off the ground and reach short-distance air speeds of up to 55 mph.
SIMILAR SPECIES: The Gould's turkey ("sky islands" in southeast) is Arizona's other, more rare, native subspecies. It's larger, with a white-tipped rump and tail feathers. The Rio Grande turkey (far northwest corner), introduced in 2008, is slightly smaller.

Merriam's turkey (male)

Gambel's quail (female, left, and male) with chicks

GAMBEL'S QUAIL

Callipepla gambelii

DESCRIPTION: Plump body; dusty gray above, buffy tan below; chestnut sides streaked white; black face; cinnamon crown; distinctive black plume; female more drab and lacks facial markings

SIZE: Length of 10 to 12 inches; wingspan of 13.5 to 14 inches; weight of 5.5 to 7 ounces

DIET: Leaves, seeds, fruits and some insects

HABITAT: Desert scrub, canyons, wooded grasslands, agricultural land and urban areas, up to 5,500 feet; prefers thorny vegetation with permanent water nearby

DISTRIBUTION: Arizona's western and southern deserts (Mohave, Sonoran and Chihuahuan)

NEST AND EGGS: Shallow depression hidden on ground; eight to 12 eggs, incubation 21 to 24 days; one or two broods

■ Gambel's are easily identified by their eye-catching plumes and familiar vocalizations, including their charming *quoit, quoit, quoit.* Through fall and winter, this gregarious species forms large groups, called coveys, of up to 40 birds. Quail are terrestrial birds. Primarily crepuscular, they emerge each morning from roosts in dense vegetation to scratch and peck before the sun is high, then resume their meal in late afternoon. Dust baths in divots of soft dirt keep skin and feathers clean. Breeders pair off in March to raise young, and reproductive success is linked to prior rainfall. The hen incubates the eggs, but the cock helps protect their precocial brood from predators, including roadrunners. Chicks begin to fly by 10 days but are not full-grown for a year. Although Gambel's quail tend to remain in their natal range, they are always on the go, frequently seen bustling single file in a fast-footed family parade.

MONTEZUMA QUAIL
Cyrtonyx montezumae

DESCRIPTION: Round shape (tail practically indiscernible); mottled black, brown and tan above; rufous below; white spots on side; bold black and white facial markings; copper crest at back of head; long, curved claws; female more pinkish brown and lacks facial markings
SIZE: Length of 8 to 9 inches; wingspan of 12 to 17 inches; weight of 4 to 8 ounces
DIET: Bulbs, acorns, seeds, berries and insects

HABITAT: Grasslands and woodlands; prefers hillsides
DISTRIBUTION: Southeastern and parts of East-Central Arizona west to Payson area
NEST AND EGGS: Shallow depression in tall grass; six to 14 eggs, incubation 25 to 26 days
■ This secretive little bird, formerly called the Mearn's quail, is a delightful find for lucky birders. Partial to life in the grasses, hidden from view, its presence is likely announced by its call, a soft *whoo* or descending trill. Although crouching motionless in camouflage is its primary protective strategy, the Montezuma quail escapes danger by exploding from the undergrowth — flushing skyward in a flurry of startled wing beats. It faces the typical threats of a ground-dwelling bird, including a long list of wild predators. But drought (which limits grass growth), overgrazing and urbanization add to this bird's challenges. Breeding season typically correlates with the summer monsoon, and nests may be built as late as August or even September. Chick-rearing is similar to the Gambel's quail.
SIMILAR SPECIES: The scaled quail (also southeast) is larger and gray-tan, with a triangular, white-tipped crest.

Montezuma quail (male)

HUMMINGBIRDS

Hummingbirds, as delicate and beautiful as the blossoms from which they feed, are unquestioned favorites among backyard naturalists. These itty-bitty birds do everything fast, with an active heart rate of up to 1,260 beats per minute. Their wings are uniquely articulated to make figure-eight strokes (40 to 90 per second), allowing stationary hovering, as well as upward, sideways and backward flight. A long tongue consumes nectar at up to 17 licks per second — but while sweet fluids feed a racing metabolism, insects provide solid nutrition. Arizona hosts around a dozen members of the hummingbird family (*Trochilidae*), although most barely enter the state or simply pass through during migration. Here, the four most prevalent species are presented, each weighing no more than a nickel. Both sexes have gem-colored plumage, but adult males also flaunt a vibrant, iridescent throat patch called a gorget. Breeding season varies but generally starts midwinter (Anna's, Costa's) or late spring (black-chinned, broad-tailed). Compact nests are soft and flexible — beautifully spun with bits of plant matter and glued with spiderwebs and cocoon silk. Mothers incubate bean-sized eggs and raise their chicks alone. Fledglings fly by three to four weeks. To conserve energy at night, hummers assume a state of temporary hibernation called torpor, dramatically lowering heart rate and body temperature until feeding can resume.

LIVING WITH WILDLIFE

Hummers found sitting still in cold weather likely are in torpor — they should be left alone but monitored for recovery. Honey readily ferments and can kill hummingbirds, so always use an appropriate sugar formula in backyard feeders. Combine one part granulated sugar with four parts water and boil for two minutes to remove impurities. Cool before using. Do not add red dye (but do use a red feeder). Feeders should be cleaned daily in the heat of a desert summer.

ANNA'S HUMMINGBIRD   *Calypte anna*

DESCRIPTION: Green above, gray belly, rose hood and gorget; female has only flecks of rose on throat center
SIZE: Length of about 4 inches; wingspan of 4.5 to 5 inches
DIET: Nectar, insects and sap (see red-naped sapsucker)
HABITAT: Woodlands, riparian areas and urban gardens
DISTRIBUTION: Year-round in Western and parts of Central and Southeastern Arizona; winter across southern two-thirds of state
NEST AND EGGS: Woven cup; two eggs, incubation 14 to 19 days; two or three broods
■ One of Arizona's largest and most vocal hummingbirds, the male Anna's emits a variety of calls, including a sharp *chee-chee-chee*. He also produces a popping sound as air flows through his tail feathers at the bottom of his courtship dive.

Anna's hummingbird (male)

Costa's hummingbird (male)

COSTA'S HUMMINGBIRD
Calypte costae

DESCRIPTION: Green above, white below, purple hood and gorget extend to points on chest; female has only purple spots on throat

SIZE: Arizona's smallest nesting bird, with length of 3.25 to 3.5 inches; wingspan of 4 to 4.5 inches

DIET: Nectar, insects and spiders

HABITAT: Desert scrub (especially washes), woodlands and urban gardens

DISTRIBUTION: Year-round in Southwestern Arizona; ranges farther north and east in summer

NEST AND EGGS: Woven cup; two eggs, incubation 15 to 18 days; rarely two broods

■ The Costa's hummingbird is a desert resident. Like other hummers, the male makes elaborate courtship dives to attract mates, potentially reaching speeds up to 50 mph.

Black-chinned hummingbird (male)

BLACK-CHINNED HUMMINGBIRD
Archilochus alexandri

DESCRIPTION: Green overall, white belly stripe, dark head, black chin, violet gorget; female has white throat and belly
SIZE: Length of 3.5 to 3.75 inches; wingspan of about 4.5 inches
DIET: Nectar and insects
HABITAT: Riparian areas, woodlands, canyons and urban gardens, below 7,700 feet
DISTRIBUTION: Statewide in spring and summer
NEST AND EGGS: Woven cup; two eggs, incubation 13 to 16 days; one to three broods
■ This "summer hummer" is commonly seen near water. Although hummingbirds do not sing, they do make a variety of chits, squeaks and trills.
SIMILAR SPECIES: The calliope hummingbird (migrates through state) has a streaked violet gorget.

BROAD-TAILED HUMMINGBIRD
Selasphorus platycercus

DESCRIPTION: Green overall, gray-white belly, white chest, red gorget, black tail; female has specked white throat and pale-orange sides
SIZE: Length of 3.25 to 4 inches; wingspan of up to 5.25 inches
DIET: Nectar, insects and spiders
HABITAT: Open woodlands, forest meadows and urban gardens; 5,200 to 9,500 feet
DISTRIBUTION: Statewide (except southwestern corner) in summer
NEST AND EGGS: Woven cup; two eggs, incubation 16 to 19 days
■ Like all hummers, the male broad-tailed hummingbird is combatively territorial. His wing beats create a cricket-like *whirr* in flight, more prominent than the expected hum.

Broad-tailed hummingbird (male, right) and rufous hummingbird

Steller's jay

STELLER'S JAY

Cyanocitta stelleri macrolopha

DESCRIPTION: Deep-blue body, wings and tail; sooty-black hood extends to gray shoulders; triangular crest; white eyebrow stripe and forehead streaks; broad, rounded wings in flight

SIZE: Length of 11 to 13 inches; wingspan of 17 to 18 inches; weight of 3.5 to 5 ounces

DIET: Acorns, nuts, seeds (especially pine), fruit, invertebrates, eggs, some small vertebrates and refuse

HABITAT: Forests, woodlands and montane campgrounds; occasionally descends to lower elevations in winter

DISTRIBUTION: All except Southwestern Arizona

NEST AND EGGS: Mud and twig cup, usually in conifer tree; three to five eggs, incubation 16 to 18 days

■ The Steller's jay, confident and inquisitive, is never hesitant to steal a snack from an unattended picnic table. It forages in the treetops and on the forest floor, often caching stores for winter. Nutshells are cracked with stabs of its sturdy bill. Like its noisy raven cousin, the jay excels at vocal mimicry, replicating the sounds of other animals and developing an assortment of calls. A social species, it normally is seen in small flocks except during nesting season. Couples share nest-building and chick-feeding responsibilities, but the female appears to

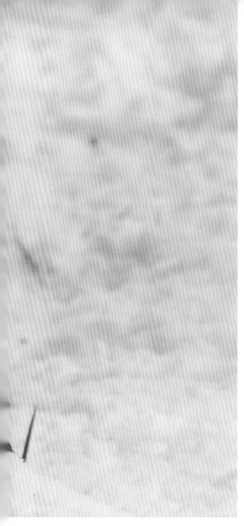

3 to 4 feet; weight of 1.5 to 3.5 pounds
DIET: Omnivorous; carrion, insects, eggs, fruits, seeds, small vertebrates and refuse
HABITAT: Almost all Arizona habitats, including urban areas
DISTRIBUTION: Statewide
NEST AND EGGS: Stick base with woven basket; three to seven eggs, incubation 20 to 25 days

■ Ravens belong to the highly intelligent *Corvidae* family (along with crows, jays and magpies). Usually seen alone or in pairs, ravens are opportunistic predators and scavengers, eating a wide array of foods, including garbage when available. Distinctively hoarse croaks may hark their passage as they flap overhead with easy wing beats. More frequently, however, ravens are seen soaring, and these aerial acrobats can execute extraordinary tricks of flight, actually flipping and tumbling on windy days. Eggs primarily are incubated by the mother, but otherwise, parents share duties. Average life span is 13 years. Along with coyotes, ravens have a rich history in Arizona's American Indian folklore.

SIMILAR SPECIES: The Chihuahuan raven (southeast) is smaller (about 20 inches) and more gregarious. The American crow (north) is smaller (about 18 inches), has a squared tail and lacks shaggy throat feathers.

handle egg incubation on her own. Jays are well known for mobbing predators — aggressively harassing, dive-bombing, even defecating on intruders — especially when protecting young.
SIMILAR SPECIES: The Western scrub-jay (statewide, except southwest), pinyon jay (north) and Mexican jay (southeast) all lack a crested black head.

COMMON RAVEN
Corvus corax

DESCRIPTION: Entirely black; long, shaggy throat feathers; long, thick bill; sturdy legs; wedge-shaped tail (contrasting a crow's straight-edged tail) most obvious in flight
SIZE: Length of 22 to 27 inches; wingspan of

Common raven

AMERICAN ROBIN
Turdus migratorius propinquus

DESCRIPTION: Gray-brown above, orange breast, white lower belly, head dark, white eye ring, yellow bill; female colors not as bold
SIZE: Length of 9 to 11 inches; wingspan of 12 to 15 inches
DIET: Earthworms, insects, fruits and berries
HABITAT: Forests, woodlands, riparian corridors and urban areas; prefers moist areas with nearby cover
DISTRIBUTION: Statewide; winters irregularly in Southwestern Arizona, year-round everywhere else
NEST AND EGGS: Cup made of dry grass and mud in tree, shrub or building eave; three or four eggs, incubation 12 to 14 days; two or three broods

■ Although it spends time plucking berries from foliage, this familiar bird is most often observed running or hopping through grass, eye cocked in search of worms. Naturally crepuscular, the American robin extends its hours during breeding season, and since males defend territories and attract females by singing, their upbeat tune — *cheerily cheer-up cheerio* — may disrupt sleepers in the wee hours of spring. Nesting occurs from April to July. About two weeks after eggs hatch, the mother may build another nest and begin incubating a new clutch while the father tends to the fledglings. Only about 25 percent will survive through fall. Like most birds, robins face threats from raptors and other predatory birds (such as ravens, jays and grackles), plus ground squirrels and snakes. A lucky few may live past six years.

MOUNTAIN BLUEBIRD
Sialia currucoides

DESCRIPTION: Sky blue overall (darker on head, wings and tail), white lower belly; dark eyes and bill; female gray overall, with wings and tail tinged blue
SIZE: Length of 6.5 to 8 inches; wingspan of 11 to 12.5 inches
DIET: Mostly insects (especially beetles and

American robin (female)

Mountain bluebird
(male)

grasshoppers); some fruits and seeds
HABITAT: Open woodlands, montane slopes, forest meadows and grasslands; occasionally agricultural areas and desert scrub
DISTRIBUTION: Statewide; year-round in north and east-central, winter irregularly everywhere else
NEST AND EGGS: Cavity (tree snag, woodpecker hole or nest box); five or six eggs, incubation 13 to 14 days; one or two broods

■ Mountain bluebirds are commonly seen perched above open terrain, ready to pounce on hapless insects or snatch them in midair. They can also hover (like kestrels), but at a much higher energy cost. In winter, these dazzling birds aggregate into conspicuous flocks, moving into lower elevations. Males head back to breeding territories by April and actively compete for nest sites; an arriving female mates with whichever male has secured the best cavity and sets to lining it with grass before laying eggs. Her doting male feeds her while she sits on the nest. With a flick of her wing, she is able to dispatch him to collect a morsel, and once chicks have hatched, she may even go so far as to beg like one of them — mouth open, wings quivering. Nestlings fledge in about three weeks but are tended for another month. If there is a second brood, offspring from the first may assist their parents.

SIMILAR SPECIES: The Western bluebird (similar range, except year-round in southeast) has a rust-colored chest and back.

Northern cardinal (male)

NORTHERN CARDINAL
Cardinalis cardinalis superbus

DESCRIPTION: Vivid red overall with prominent crest; black face and chin; orange, cone-shaped bill; dark eyes; female taupe, with red tones on crest, wings and tail, and light-gray face
SIZE: Length of 8 to 9 inches; wingspan of 10 to 12 inches
DIET: Seeds, invertebrates and fruits
HABITAT: Desert scrub, wooded canyons and urban areas
DISTRIBUTION: Year-round in West-Central to Southeastern Arizona
NEST AND EGGS: Twig cup in dense shrubs; three or four eggs, incubation 11 to 13 days; up to four broods

■ Cardinals in the desert? Yes — in summer pairs or winter family flocks. And this Southwestern subspecies is noticeably larger than the eastern variety, capturing the attention of all who glimpse it. Both sexes sing year-round, a variable string of clear whistles. But a single, sharp *chip* is their most common call. Obsessively territorial in spring and early summer, a northern cardinal may attack its own reflection in a window. Chicks, fed by both parents, fledge about nine days after hatching and are independent after one and a half months. Like the American robin, a cardinal mother may leave fledgling care to her mate while she begins incubating the next clutch of eggs. Many sports fans adore this bird — in 1988, an NFL football team, now known as the Arizona Cardinals, relocated to the desert.
SIMILAR SPECIES: The male summer tanager (nearly statewide in summer) is another all-red bird but lacks a pointy crest and black mask. The pyrrhuloxia, sometimes called a "desert cardinal" (south), resembles a female cardinal but is gray, with red accents on face, crest, chest, wings and tail, and a pale-yellow bill.

WESTERN TANAGER
Piranga ludoviciana

DESCRIPTION: Bright-yellow body, black wings with yellow and white bars, black tail, red head (summer only); short, thick bill; female yellow-gray above, yellow-green below
SIZE: Length of 6.5 to 7.5 inches; wingspan of 11 to 12 inches
DIET: Insects and fruits
HABITAT: Forests and woodlands
DISTRIBUTION: Summers in Northern and Eastern Arizona; migrates through rest of state
NEST AND EGGS: Woven cup in coniferous tree; three or four eggs, incubation about 13 days

■ This strictly arboreal species spends its days high in the canopy, hopping between branches. Being somewhat difficult to spot makes its red-and-yellow flash all the more rewarding to see. Unlike certain other colorful species (like the house finch) that get seasonal red pigment from eating plants, the Western tanager presumably obtains pigment from eating insects that eat plants. Although the female builds the nest and incubates the eggs, her mate remains close, guarding her and sometimes bringing food. Both sexes feed and tend nestlings. Fledglings exit the nest at 11 to 15 days but stay with their parents two to four weeks longer. Like all passerines (also known as perching birds), tanagers have three toes pointing forward and one toe back.

Western tanager (male)

Curve-billed thrasher

CURVE-BILLED THRASHER
Toxostoma curvirostre palmeri

DESCRIPTION: Stocky; gray-brown overall with diffuse mottling on chest; long, dark bill curves down; yellow-orange eyes
SIZE: Length of 10 to 12 inches; wingspan of 13 to 14 inches
DIET: Mostly invertebrates (especially beetles); some fruits and seeds
HABITAT: Desert scrub, grasslands, woodlands and urban areas
DISTRIBUTION: Southern (except extreme southwest) and West-Central Arizona
NEST AND EGGS: Loose, deep cup, frequently in cholla cactus; two to four eggs, incubation 12 to 15 days; two or three broods

■ This spry bird is a familiar sight and sound among the cactuses and mesquite trees of the Sonoran Desert. Its call is a *whit-wheet*. Using its prominent arched bill, it tosses aside leaf litter and probes the dirt for food. Although nesting may begin as early as January, the majority of eggs are laid from March to May, and both sexes incubate and care for young. Curve-billed thrashers reach maturity at a year old, and while mortality is high in chicks and juveniles, adults have a fairly good survival rate. They have been recorded living more than 10 years.
SIMILAR SPECIES: The Bendire's thrasher (parts of south and migrates north) has brown bars on its chest and a straighter bill. The crissal thrasher (most of state) is fairly secretive, with rust plumage under its tail base, a dark whisker streak and an extremely curved bill.

NORTHERN MOCKINGBIRD
Mimus polyglottos

DESCRIPTION: Silver-gray above, cream below, darker wings and tail, yellow eyes, black bill; wing feathers tipped white; large white wing patches and white outer-tail feathers visible in flight

SIZE: Length of 8 to 11 inches; wingspan of 12 to 15 inches; male larger than female

DIET: Invertebrates (mostly insects) and fruits

HABITAT: Desert scrub, grasslands, open woodlands, forest edges and urban areas, up to 7,800 feet

DISTRIBUTION: Statewide; more common in northeast during summer

NEST AND EGGS: Male builds twig foundation, while female adds cup in dense shrub or cactus; four or five eggs, incubation 12 to 13 days; two or three broods

■ *Polyglottos* means "many voices." Indeed, this bird is a first-rate mimic — a mockingbird can sound like a dozen species by artfully imitating their tunes in lengthy repetition, and a male will learn up to 200 songs in his lifetime. Unmated, he may sing through the night in spring. Busybodies by nature, northern mockingbirds forage while walking or running on the ground, occasionally flashing their wing patches or flitting up and down from elevated perches. Chasing is commonplace in both courtship and territorial displays, and mockingbirds are quick to mob any perceived intruder. Breeding begins in late winter. The mother incubates the eggs, but chicks are fed by both parents and leave the nest within a couple of weeks.

SIMILAR SPECIES: The loggerhead shrike (statewide) has a black eye stripe. The sage thrasher (north in summer, south in winter) lacks wing patches and has more striped plumage. The Townsend's solitaire (year-round in northeast, central and southeast in winter) is bland gray with a white eye ring.

LIVING WITH WILDLIFE

Make your yard a wildlife haven. Plant native trees and flowers to attract birds and butterflies. A water source — pond or birdbath — is a great addition. Be sure to keep it fresh for your visitors. Grains and seeds are the best all-purpose fare for feeders. Add suet in the winter and fresh sliced fruit in the summer to keep the birds coming year-round.

Northern mockingbird

CACTUS WREN
Campylorhynchus brunneicapillus

DESCRIPTION: Streaked and barred brown above, streaked white below, dark spotting on throat, chocolate crown, characteristic white eyebrow stripe; long bill has slight downward curve
SIZE: Arizona's largest wren, with length of 7 to 8.5 inches; wingspan of 10.5 to 11 inches
DIET: Mostly insects and spiders; some fruits and seeds; occasional nectar
HABITAT: Desert scrub and associated urban areas
DISTRIBUTION: Half of Arizona, across Mohave, Sonoran and Chihuahuan deserts
NEST AND EGGS: Football-shaped grass and weed shell, with tubular entrance in dense, thorny vegetation; three or four eggs, incubation about 16 days; two or three broods

▪ The cactus wren was designated Arizona's state bird in 1931. With a pronounced voice of progressively louder notes — *char char char char char!* — and a distinctive appearance, it is easily spotted within its range. This desert resident does not require free-standing water, flipping rocks and other objects in search of prey from which to gain moisture. During evening dust baths, the cactus wren rubs and kicks dirt into its feathers to dislodge parasites. This species defends its territory year-round, readily mobbing intruders, and will even destroy other birds' nests. The male's own nests are frequently constructed amid the protective spines of cholla cactuses, yet may still be predated by coachwhip snakes. Breeding season is quite long (February to August). As courtship, the male cactus wren crouches and growls at his mate. In the time she incubates their eggs, he will build a new nest for their next brood — and possibly some decoy nests, too. Both parents participate in chick-rearing and give parental assistance for at least six weeks. Empty nests are used for roosting.
SIMILAR SPECIES: The sage thrasher (year-round in northeast, south in winter) lacks a dark crown and white eyebrow stripe. The canyon wren (statewide) has a specked cinnamon body and a white throat. The rock wren (statewide) is dull gray above and buffy below, with rust near its rump.

Cactus wren

Great-tailed grackle (female)

GREAT-TAILED GRACKLE
Quiscalus mexicanus

DESCRIPTION: Iridescent purple-black overall; bold yellow eyes; large, pointed bill; extremely long, keel-shaped tail; female has coppery brown head and belly; not to be confused with the dark-eyed brown-headed cowbird
SIZE: Length of 15 to 18 inches; wingspan of 19 to 23 inches; weight of 4 to 7 ounces; male larger than female
DIET: Opportunistic omnivore; invertebrates, amphibians, fish, small vertebrates (nest raider), seeds, fruits, carrion and refuse
HABITAT: Most Arizona habitats, including urban areas; requires nearby water; up to 7,500 feet
DISTRIBUTION: Statewide; northern birds may move southward in winter
NEST AND EGGS: Colonial; bulky cup, lined with mud and grass, in tree; three or four eggs, incubation 13 to 14 days; one or two broods

■ Like most perching birds, grackles are diurnal. And this is one of the most conspicuous avian species in public areas — gregarious flocks incessantly chatter in brash whistles and creaks, often begging or stealing unattended foodstuffs. Natural foraging is done on the ground or in shallow water, providing a highly variable diet. Male great-tailed grackles are markedly flamboyant. They make threat displays by arching their neck, so their bill is pointed straight up. They strut about, feathers fluffed and wings akimbo, when courting females. These brash boys mate with many females (February to July), and while mothers raise offspring alone, they have the company of a loose colony. Chicks fledge after three weeks but require an additional two weeks before they fly well.
SIMILAR SPECIES: The male Brewer's blackbird (year-round in northeast; rest of state in winter) is smaller and solid black; it has yellow eyes but lacks a long, keeled tail.

BROWN-HEADED COWBIRD
Molothrus ater

DESCRIPTION: Stocky build; shiny green-black, with brown head; dark eyes; lacks yellow eyes and long tail of female great-tailed grackle; female dull brown overall
SIZE: Length of 6.5 to 8.5 inches; wingspan of 13 to 15 inches; weight of 1 to 2 ounces
DIET: Seeds, invertebrates and some eggs (when invading nests)
HABITAT: Forest edges, open woodlands, grasslands, urban parks and horse pastures
DISTRIBUTION: Statewide; year-round in

Brown-headed cowbirds
(female, top, and male)

Red-winged
blackbird (male)

Southern Arizona, summers everywhere else
NEST AND EGGS: No nest; one to seven eggs laid singly in other passerine species' nests, incubation 10 to 12 days

■ The brown-headed cowbird is a notorious brood parasite. One female may lay more than 40 eggs per season (April to July) in the nests of other birds. Because a cowbird chick hatches relatively soon, it gains a head start, often elbowing out rival eggs or nestlings. During its growth phase, it readily adapts to the lifestyle and diet of its foster parent(s). Some birds recognize and discard cowbird eggs, but most don't — at least 139 passerine species have been duped into raising a cowbird chick. As adults, cowbirds primarily forage on the ground in tight flocks. They earned their common name by trailing grazers, such as cattle.

SIMILAR SPECIES: The male bronzed cowbird (migratory in most of south) is solid black, with red eyes. The male Brewer's blackbird (breeds in northeast; west and south in winter) is solid black, with yellow eyes.

RED-WINGED BLACKBIRD
Agelaius phoeniceus

DESCRIPTION: Glossy black, with red and yellow shoulder patches (more prominent in breeding season); female streaked brown,

with dark eye stripe, pale eyebrow and possible red tinge to face or shoulders
SIZE: Length of 7 to 9 inches; wingspan of 12 to 15 inches
DIET: Seeds and invertebrates (mostly insects)
HABITAT: Montane wetlands, riparian corridors, lowland marshes and agricultural areas
DISTRIBUTION: Statewide
NEST AND EGGS: Stringy cup stems hidden in reeds or cattails; two to four eggs, incubation 11 to 13 days

■ The male red-winged blackbird can't be missed or mistaken with his vibrant epaulettes, which decorate summer marshes. *Conk-la-reee!* he sings across the water. Each male supports several females (up to 15) in his breeding territory. There, he perches high in the cattails, scouting competition and attacking intruders. After mating (not always with the territory holder), a mother incubates her eggs alone, though the male occasionally assists with the feeding of chicks, which leave the nest by two weeks of age. In winter, immense flocks aggregate in fields and pastures, mixing with grackles and cowbirds. It is said that the average life span for any bird in the wild is about one and a half years; in addition to predation, birds may succumb to parasites, starvation or disease. However, with success, this species can survive more than 14 years.

Phainopepla (male)

PHAINOPEPLA

Phainopepla nitens

DESCRIPTION: Slender build; glossy black overall, with conspicuous white patch on flight feathers visible in flight; female gray overall, with white margins on dorsal wing feathers; both sexes have wispy crest, red eyes, short black bill and long tail
SIZE: Length of 7 to 8 inches; wingspan of 11 to 12 inches
DIET: Mostly mistletoe berries and insects
HABITAT: Desert scrub, woodlands and riparian areas; prefers areas with mistletoe
DISTRIBUTION: Winters in southwest; moves north and east in summer

NEST AND EGGS: Cup with twigs, spiderwebs and animal hair, usually in mistletoe cluster; two or three eggs, incubation 14 to 16 days; one or two broods

■ On occasion, the phainopepla — Greek for "shining robe" — is conjectured to be a black cardinal, which doesn't exist. But once familiar, it is an easy-to-identify species that tends to perch on the highest branches. Its song is complex, but it can also mimic other birds. Males perform courtship displays, including aerial circles and zigzags, resulting in monogamous couplings. Nesting behavior is quite unique: Some phainopeplas actually migrate between broods. In February, a nest is built in the Sonoran Desert, where pairs react with territorial vigor to protect their nest and associated clumps of fruit-laden mistletoe. Around May, couples may move and raise a second brood in cooler woodlands, where they nest in a more colonial fashion. Parents work as a team to incubate eggs, later feeding chicks insects and crushed berries. Fledging occurs after two to three weeks. Since the phainopepla feeds heavily on mistletoe berries (up to 1,100 per day), it aids in spreading the parasitic plant's seeds through its sticky excrement.

WHITE-BREASTED NUTHATCH
Sitta carolinensis

DESCRIPTION: Distinctive thick-necked shape; blue-gray above, white face and breast, black crown, chestnut smudge under rump; narrow bill slightly upturned; short tail; characteristically forages and perches head-down on tree trunks, neck craned outward
SIZE: Length of 5 to 6 inches; wingspan of 8 to 10.5 inches; weight of 0.6 to 1 ounce

DIET: Insects, spiders and seeds; some acorns and nuts
HABITAT: Woodlands, forests, riparian corridors and urban areas
DISTRIBUTION: Eastern and Northern Arizona
NEST AND EGGS: Lined cavity (tree or woodpecker hole); five to nine eggs, incubation 12 to 14 days
■ These cute little birds have supreme clinging skills. They can hop headfirst down vertical surfaces. Or sideways. Or even upside-down under thick limbs. Nuts and seeds are jammed into wood cracks and "hatched" open with a sharp bill — thus the name. White-breasted nuthatches live in pairs throughout the year, nesting from March to July. The female incubates, but her mate helps feed young. Winter flocks often forage with other small birds, visiting backyard feeders to collect stores, which are cached in bark crevices, typically hidden by some type of covering like lichen. Their most common call is a nasal *auk-auk-auk*.
SIMILAR SPECIES: The pygmy nuthatch (similar range) is smaller, with a gray-brown cap and a dark eye stripe. The red-breasted nuthatch (year-round in east and north) has pale-orange underparts and black and white facial stripes.

White-breasted nuthatch

Say's phoebe

SAY'S PHOEBE
Sayornis saya

DESCRIPTION: Pale gray-brown overall; tawny lower belly; long, dark tail; slight peak to head
SIZE: Length of 7 to 8 inches; wingspan of 12 to 13 inches
DIET: Insects; occasional spiders; rarely berries
HABITAT: Desert scrub, grasslands, agricultural land and urban areas
DISTRIBUTION: Statewide; year-round in Southern and Western Arizona, summers everywhere else
NEST AND EGGS: Cup on covered ledge of cave, building or bridge; four or five eggs, incubation 12 to 14 days; up to three broods
■ Phoebes are a type of flycatcher, known for pumping their tail while perched. They often make short flights to capture insects on the wing, returning to the same perch over and over again. They can also hover to glean meals off vegetation. Say's phoebes may usurp old barn-swallow nests if available. Their primary song is *pit-eur.*
SIMILAR SPECIES: The female vermilion flycatcher (year-round in south, parts of central in summer) has a whitish throat, orange lower belly and streaked chest. The ash-throated flycatcher (nearly statewide in summer) is white below and has rusty accents on its wings and tail.

BLACK PHOEBE
Sayornis nigricans

DESCRIPTION: Black overall, with white mid-lower belly; slight peak to head
SIZE: Length of 6 to 7 inches; wingspan of 10.5 to 11 inches
DIET: Mostly insects; some small fish
HABITAT: Open woodlands, desert canyons, agricultural land and urban areas; almost always near water
DISTRIBUTION: Year-round along angled bar from West-Central to Southeastern Arizona; winters in southwest; summers in northwest and east-central regions
NEST AND EGGS: Mud and fiber shell on vertical wall; four or five eggs, incubation 15 to 18 days; up to three broods
■ The black phoebe's *tsip* call may be heard in the vicinity of waterways and marshes. In addition to foraging like Say's phoebes, black phoebes sometimes catch minnows from the water surface, where they feed. It is believed that the female phoebe builds the nest after being shown several potential sites by the male. Primarily monogamous, incubation is done by the mother, but both parents feed chicks. They fledge the nest in two to three weeks.

Black phoebe

Verdin

VERDIN

Auriparus flaviceps

DESCRIPTION: Dusty gray overall; yellowish-green head; small, red shoulder patch; fine-pointed bill; female slightly muted
SIZE: Length of 3.5 to 4.5 inches; wingspan of 6.5 to 7 inches; weight of about 0.25 ounces
DIET: Insects (including larvae and eggs), small spiders, nectar, berries, fruits and some seeds
HABITAT: Desert scrub, open woodlands and urban areas
DISTRIBUTION: Central, Southern and far Western Arizona
NEST AND EGGS: Bulky, oval stick shell; usually four eggs, incubation 10 to 14 days; one or two broods

■ Perhaps unfamiliar to a casual observer, this tiny, sprightly bird is characteristic of the desert.

Flitting among the thickets, sometimes hanging upside down, it forages insects and nips nectar from the base of blossoms. A staccato *tschep*, often repeated, gives it away in dense foliage. Verdins are even more prolific nest builders than cactus wrens — and in equally thorny locations. They craft roosting nests year-round. And when a mating pair bonds in spring, the male constructs several (up to 11 recorded) brooding nests from which the female can choose. Although the mother incubates the eggs alone, the male will help feed their chicks. Fledglings leave the nest at about 17 to 21 days old but return to their natal nest each night for some length of time before attempting to fabricate their own roosting quarters. Despite their small size, verdins are vocal and conspicuous.

House finches
(female, left, and male)

HOUSE FINCH

Haemorhous mexicanus

DESCRIPTION: Brown above, heavily streaked brown and cream below, brown crown, rosy red face and bib (an uncommon variant has orange or yellow in place of red); short, conical bill; female lacks colorful head
SIZE: Length of 5 to 6 inches; wingspan of 8 to 10 inches
DIET: Seeds, buds and fruits
HABITAT: Almost all Arizona habitats (especially common in urban areas)
DISTRIBUTION: Statewide
NEST AND EGGS: Woven cup in tree, cactus or building; three to five eggs, incubation 13 to 14 days; up to three broods

■ Backyard naturalists know these birds well, as they are often the most plentiful species at the feeder. Beloved for their gregarious nature and cheerful, warbling song, monogamous pairs begin mating in late winter, with eggs in the nest as early as February. With feedings from both parents, hatchlings become fledglings in 12 to 15 days. House finches are clearly adaptable to human habitats, but increases of viral and parasitic disease have been documented in urbanized settings.
SIMILAR SPECIES: The Cassin's finch (year-round in north) has a red, not brown, cap with a pinkish face and breast.

CLIFF SWALLOW
Petrochelidon pyrrhonota

DESCRIPTION: Brown-black wings, back, tail and crown; white belly; rufous throat; ochre forehead, neck and rump; short, square tail and pointed wings particularly noticeable in flight

SIZE: Length of 5 to 6 inches; wingspan of 11 to 13 inches

DIET: Flying insects

HABITAT: Canyon cliffs, river valleys, urban bridges and agricultural areas; requires nearby mud for nest construction, so typically found near water source

DISTRIBUTION: Most of Arizona in summer; migrates through southwestern corner

NEST AND EGGS: Colonial; mud gourd protected by overhang; four or five eggs, incubation 14 to 16 days

■ These widespread summer swallows are a real pleasure to observe. Busy flocks can be spotted circling overhead (gobbling insect swarms), zipping and dipping over waterways or darting from under bridges, where hundreds of active nests may be found from March to July. Both sexes incubate and care for chicks, which timidly peek from their nest holes before fledging at three to four weeks. Curiously, a female cliff swallow sometimes carries one of her eggs in her bill to stick in another swallow's nest.

SIMILAR SPECIES: The barn swallow (summers in central and east, migrates across rest of state) is blue above and cinnamon below, with a deeply forked tail.

Cliff swallow

Violet-green swallow

VIOLET-GREEN SWALLOW
Tachycineta thalassina

DESCRIPTION: Emerald-green back and crown; dark (violet) wings and tail; white face, belly and rump patches; short, notched tail; female coloring more dull

SIZE: Length of 5 to 5.5 inches; wingspan of 10 to 12 inches

DIET: Flying insects

HABITAT: Open woodlands, forests, canyons and urban areas

DISTRIBUTION: Most of Arizona in summer; migrates through southwestern corner

NEST AND EGGS: Twig cup in tree cavity, rock crevice or nest box; four to six eggs, incubation 13 to 18 days

■ This little Western swallow is a talented aerialist with a fluttery flight style perfect for capturing airborne prey. Violet-greens are not as social as cliff swallows, although they do forage in flocks. Breeding season and nestling care are fairly similar, except the mother violet-green incubates eggs alone. Both species make high-pitched tweets and cheeps.

SIMILAR SPECIES: The tree swallow (northeast in summer) has dark-blue upper parts that extend below its eyes. The white-throated swift (year-round in south, summers in north) has longer, narrower wings and black patches on its belly.

Greater roadrunner

GREATER ROADRUNNER

Geococcyx californianus

DESCRIPTION: Lean frame; heavily streaked tan, dark brown and white; pale belly; blue-and-orange skin patch behind yellow eye; bushy crest; extremely long tail; wings appear rounded in flight

SIZE: Length of 20 to 24 inches; wingspan of 1.5 to 2 feet; weight of 8 to 12 ounces

DIET: Lizards, snakes, birds, invertebrates and rodents; some fruits and seeds

HABITAT: Desert scrub, grasslands, woodlands and urban areas; prefers open terrain with scattered cover

DISTRIBUTION: Most of Arizona (sparingly north of Mogollon Rim)

NEST AND EGGS: Twig cup in tree, bush or cactus; three to five eggs, incubation about 20 days

■ Arizona's most legendary bird is touted as a coyote-escaping, rattler-fighting speed demon. For the record, the greater roadrunner is not blue and does not say *beep-beep* (it actually coos like a dove). Still, it lives up to much of its

hype. This charismatic bird can fly but rarely does. Darting forward, tail parallel to the ground and head outstretched, it appears perfectly streamlined. At a standstill, it expressively flicks its tail and perks its crest. Like all members of its cuckoo family (*Cuculidae*), the roadrunner is zygodactyl, and its toe configuration supports running speeds up to 15 mph. Being swift afoot helps this diurnal animal not only dodge predators but also catch prey, including the occasional rattlesnake. And it can leap straight up to snatch flying birds out of the air. Breeding pairs, which may be monogamous, engage in courtship rituals that include gift-giving — natural trinkets or food items — and both sexes are active parents, including during incubation. After chicks fledge at three weeks, they continue to be fed by their parents for another four to six weeks while they hone their hunting skills. On cold mornings, roadrunners warm up by lifting their back feathers and exposing black skin to the sun. Another intriguing adaptation: Since water is scarce in the desert, they can excrete concentrated salt through glands near their eyes (like seabirds do). They occasionally perch on fence posts or telephone wires.

DUCKS

Arizona attracts more than 35 species from the family *Anatidae*, which comprises ducks, swans and geese. Sturdy fliers, these water birds typically migrate north to summer nesting grounds and south to warmer wintering grounds. Many are seasonal visitors to Arizona from November to March. There are two types of ducks: dabbling and diving. Dabbling ducks eat near the water surface and, even when upended, are always in view. They can take flight directly off the water. Diving ducks forage deeper down, disappearing from the surface for seconds at a time. They must run and flap over the water before lifting into the sky. All anatids have feathers that are waterproofed with special oils, and all have webbed feet to aid in swimming and strong, flat bills to pluck aquatic vegetation and/or filter organisms from their watery environment. Most species exhibit sexual dimorphism. The mother alone incubates the eggs in a dry nest and cares for her precocial brood. Ducks are preyed upon by many animals but are also extremely vulnerable to human impacts, including water pollution and fishing-line entanglement. A group of floating anatids is cleverly called a raft.

BUFFLEHEAD
Bucephala albeola

DESCRIPTION: Petite build; glossy black (purple-green iridescent) above, white below; puffy, round head has large, bonnet-like white patch; short, gray-blue bill; white patch on upper wing visible in flight; female more gray-brown, with white cheek patch
SIZE: Arizona's smallest diving duck, with length of 13 to 15 inches; wingspan of 1.5 to 2 feet
DIET: Aquatic invertebrates (including dragonfly larvae), snails and some seeds
HABITAT: Lakes, rivers and ponds
DISTRIBUTION: Statewide in winter
NEST AND EGGS: Cavity (northern flicker hole or nest box); eight to 10 eggs, incubation 28 to 33 days
■ This diving duck, with its unique shape and bold coloring, is a special treat to spy. Not very gregarious, it tends to be found in groups of

fewer than 10. Unlike some ducks that spend time ashore, buffleheads live almost exclusively on water. Monogamous pairs may stay together for several breeding seasons, and their offspring do not reach sexual maturity for two years.

Common mergansers (females)

COMMON MERGANSER
Mergus merganser

DESCRIPTION: Streamlined appearance; gray and black above, white below; black-green head with red, hook-tipped bill; orange-red legs; white patches on upper wings visible in flight; female grayish overall, with white chin and chest, and rust-colored head with short crest at back
SIZE: Length of 22 to 27 inches; wingspan of 2.5 to 3 feet
DIET: Primarily small fish; occasional insects, frogs and plant matter
HABITAT: Rivers, lakes and ponds
DISTRIBUTION: Statewide; year-round along

Buffleheads (male, left, and female)

Mogollon Rim and Verde River, winters everywhere else
NEST AND EGGS: Crevice lined with leaves and feathers; nine to 12 eggs, incubation 28 to 35 days

■ This commonly seen diving duck forms large flocks on open water, often mixed in with other species. Its nickname is "Sawtooth" — mergansers have a long, narrow bill, serrated to grip prey, that is notably different from other ducks. So is the striking plumage of the female. Some common mergansers stay and breed at higher elevations in Arizona.

RING-NECKED DUCK
Aythya collaris

DESCRIPTION: Black chest, back and tail; gray sides; white belly; dark-purple head, slightly crested to a peak; bill is tri-colored (black, white and gray); golden eyes; female brown overall, with gray head, buffy around base of bill and eyes, and dark iris
SIZE: Length of 15 to 18 inches; wingspan of about 2 feet
DIET: Aquatic plants and invertebrates
HABITAT: Marshes, lakes, rivers, ponds and stock tanks
DISTRIBUTION: Statewide; year-round in far east-central, winters everywhere else
NEST AND EGGS: Simple grass-and-moss bowl near water, sometimes on floating vegetation; eight to 10 eggs, incubation 25 to 29 days

■ This bird's name doesn't seem to fit — that's because it is nearly impossible to make out the chestnut ring on its black neck. Although a diver,

Ring-necked duck (male)

a ring-necked duck will sometime dabble at the surface, and large winter flocks often form in Arizona wetlands.
SIMILAR SPECIES: The lesser scaup (statewide in winter) has a pale-gray saddle and a blue bill.

American wigeon (male)

AMERICAN WIGEON
Anas americana

DESCRIPTION: Ruddy gray overall; white crown; iridescent green patch sweeps back from eye to nape; small, pale-blue bill with black tip; white-and-green patch on upper wing visible in flight; female reddish overall, with gray-brown head
SIZE: Length of 18 to 23 inches; wingspan of 2.5 to 3 feet
DIET: Mostly aquatic plants and grasses; some insects
HABITAT: Rivers, lakes, stock tanks and ponds; also grazes urban parks and golf courses
DISTRIBUTION: Statewide in winter
NEST AND EGGS: Grass bowl, lined with down, on ground among tall grass; seven to 10 eggs, incubation 22 to 25 days

■ This dabbling duck prefers to forage in shallower waters or on the ground in grassy fields. It is often associated with diving water birds, including coots, which stir up the water and raise plant matter to the surface. Limited breeding has been documented in the White Mountains.

Great blue herons

GREAT BLUE HERON

Ardea herodias

DESCRIPTION: Tall, lanky frame; bluish gray overall; shaggy plumes on wings and sinewy neck in breeding season; slender white face; black eye stripes extend back into plumes; pointed yellow bill; long, dark legs

SIZE: Height of 3.5 to 4.5 feet; wingspan of 5.5 to 6.5 feet; weight of 5 to 6 pounds

DIET: Mostly fish; some small mammals, amphibians, birds, reptiles and invertebrates

HABITAT: Lakeshores, riverbanks, marshes and urban ponds; occasionally grasslands and agricultural land

DISTRIBUTION: Statewide

NEST AND EGGS: Colonial; bulky stick platform, usually in treetop; three to five eggs, incubation 25 to 30 days; one brood

■ This majestic wading bird is a solitary, crepuscular hunter, methodically stalking prey on stilted legs. Before its daggered bill strikes, the great blue heron poises motionless, silhouette often mirrored on the water's edge. Commonly found in urban parks, it emits a raspy squawk when disturbed by passers-by. And flying overhead, it resembles a prehistoric pterodactyl with slow, steady wing beats, neck tucked and legs trailing behind. Nesting colonies in Arizona seldom surpass 50 pairs. The male gathers materials for the female to weave, and they share parenting duties. Chicks, which are fed by regurgitation, fledge after two to three months and reach maturity in two years.

SIMILAR SPECIES: The sandhill crane (parts of south in winter) has a red cap and a smaller, black beak, and it flies with its neck outstretched.

SNOWY EGRET

Egretta thula

DESCRIPTION: White plumage; black, dagger-like bill; skinny black legs; bright-yellow feet; in breeding season, lacy plumes on head, chest and rump, plus feet and skin in front of eye (lore) turn red-orange
SIZE: Height of about 2 feet; wingspan of about 3.5 feet; weight of up to 1 pound
DIET: Small fish, amphibians and invertebrates
HABITAT: Marshes, ponds, rivers and occasionally irrigated fields
DISTRIBUTION: Year-round in Central and Western Arizona; statewide during migration
NEST AND EGGS: Colonial; stick platform in low shrubs or on ground; two to four eggs, incubation 20 to 24 days

■ Egrets are in the heron family (*Ardeidae*). The snowy egret feeds in the shallows, but unlike the steady great blue heron, it actively probes and shuffles to stir up prey. A savvy hunter,

it can also hover above the water. Several heron species, including the snowy egret, have been documented bait-fishing — employing an object or piece of food to lure fish within striking distance. It's an impressive example of tool use. Egrets frequently mix with other water birds and nest in colonies. Both parents care for chicks. In the 1800s, the snowy egret's gorgeous plumes decorated women's hats at a cost higher than that of gold. Increasing demand drove this species to the brink of extinction before it gained protection under the Migratory Bird Treaty Act of 1918. Thankfully, its numbers have finally recovered.

SIMILAR SPECIES: The great egret is much larger (3.5 feet tall), with black legs and feet, and a yellow bill. The cattle egret (central and southwest) is slightly smaller, with yellow legs and a yellow bill; it develops patches of pale-orange plumage during breeding season.

Snowy egret

American coot

AMERICAN COOT
Fulica americana

DESCRIPTION: Round-bodied; slate gray overall; pointed white bill has maroon (or white) forehead shield and dark ring at tip; yellow-green legs; lobed toes; dark-red eyes; young chick has ornamental coloration (black with orange-tipped down and bare pink crown and bill)
SIZE: Length of 13 to 17 inches; wingspan of about 2 feet
DIET: Aquatic and terrestrial plants and seeds, invertebrates, small fishes and tadpoles
HABITAT: Marshes, lakes, rivers and urban-park ponds
DISTRIBUTION: Statewide
NEST AND EGGS: Several woven baskets on floating platform anchored to stand of reeds or grasses; six to 11 eggs, incubation 21 to 25 days; one or two broods

■ Coots do not have webbed feet; rather, they have scalloped toes for paddling. Sizable flocks dive, dabble or graze on land in a cacophony of clucks. They often gather with other water birds, sometimes pirating food. Both sexes partake in incubation and chick-rearing, but females may also lay eggs in other coots' nests. This sneaky behavior does not always pay off: Studies show coots can count and recognize their own eggs and will push aside unwelcome additions.
SIMILAR SPECIES: The common moorhen, or gallinule (Southern and Western Arizona), has a red bill with a yellow tip.

WESTERN GREBE
Aechmophorus occidentalis

DESCRIPTION: Sharply two-toned; black-gray above, white below; black crown extends down over red eye; swan-like neck; long, slender, greenish-yellow bill
SIZE: Length of 22 to 29 inches; wingspan of 2 to 2.5 feet
DIET: Small fish, aquatic invertebrates and feathers (yes, grebes are known for this)
HABITAT: Lakes, ponds and marshes
DISTRIBUTION: Year-round along Colorado River and in some central reservoirs; winters and migration elsewhere
NEST AND EGGS: Colonial; mounds of floating vegetation anchored to aquatic or flooded plants; two to four eggs, incubation 24 days on average

■ Grebes have broad lobes on their toes (not scalloped like coots), and their legs are set far back on their bodies, rendering them clumsy afoot. Thus, they are almost never on land. Strong underwater swimmers, these predators can thrust their head forward, potentially spearing prey, as herons do. The characteristic *kreet-kreet* of the Western grebe is a favored summer sound. But this bird is perhaps most loved for its synchronized courtship dance — pairs posture, chest high, holding weeds or running side by side over the water surface in an elegant ballet. Young chicks often ride on the back of a parent.
SIMILAR SPECIES: The Clark's grebe (similar range) appears almost identical but has a yellow-orange bill, and its black crown does not extend down to its cheek, so the eye is in the white zone.

Western grebes

📷 TOP: GEORGE ANDREJKO, ARIZONA GAME AND FISH DEPARTMENT ABOVE: DONAL HILL

Killdeer

KILLDEER

Charadrius vociferus

DESCRIPTION: Brown above, white below, cinnamon rump; two distinguishing black bands on chest; dark and light facial stripes; orange-red eyes; pale, lanky legs; long tail; wings slender and pointed in flight
SIZE: Length of 8 to 11 inches; wingspan of about 1.5 feet
DIET: Invertebrates (mostly insects; some worms, snails and larvae)
HABITAT: Wetlands, riverbanks, fields, agricultural land and urban areas; prefers sparse or no vegetation
DISTRIBUTION: Statewide
NEST AND EGGS: Many scrapes made on open ground before choosing one to line with pebbles and debris; three to five eggs, incubation 24 to 28 days; two broods

■ This is a type of plover, officially a shorebird. But even with long legs for wading and pretty good swimming skills, the killdeer is often found far from water. It has a quirky way of darting and halting while searching for food, regularly emitting its namesake shriek — *kil-dee!* Mating pairs carry out a scrape-making ceremony together, and after egg-laying, the father assumes the night shift for incubation. A killdeer parent employs several methods to protect its developing brood. It might pretend to incubate an empty nest, or it might fluff its feathers, lift its tail over its head and charge at an obtuse ungulate with clumsy hooves. If necessary, the killdeer performs a convincing broken-wing act, drawing a dangerous predator away from the vicinity before hastily taking flight. While still relatively common, populations appear to be in slow decline — living close to humans, these birds are exposed to pesticides, machinery (cars and lawn mowers) and domestic predators (dogs and cats). Their flight is marked by stiff and intermittent wing beats.

REPTILES

Desert spiny lizard

Sonoran Desert tortoise

SONORAN DESERT TORTOISE
Gopherus morafkai

DESCRIPTION: Domed carapace with growth rings on scales (scutes); varied coloration from dark gray-brown to olive-gray; flattened and shovel-like front legs with nails for digging; elephant-like back legs
LENGTH: Less than 15 inches
DIET: Plants, grasses and cactuses
HABITAT: Desert scrub (especially rocky bajadas and washes); occasionally grasslands and woodlands
DISTRIBUTION: Sonoran and Mohave deserts south and east of the Colorado River
CONSERVATION STATUS: *Gopherus morafkai* was recently separated from the threatened *Gopherus agassizii* (now called Agassiz's desert tortoise), which occurs north and west of the Colorado River. The tortoise is managed and protected in Arizona.

■ Tortoises are land turtles. The Sonoran Desert tortoise is rarely seen because it spends the majority of its life in shelters that it excavates, protected from the extreme temperatures of the desert. Most active from the summer monsoon season into early fall, this terrestrial reptile forages by day and can go a year without drinking. Females mature at 12 to 20 years old and lay a clutch of up to 12 eggs every one to two years. Like most turtles, the desert tortoise can pull its head and legs into its shell for protection. Still, many animals prey upon youngsters. Even adult tortoises sporting hefty, durable shells are eaten by mountain lions. The greatest threat to this species, however, is not predation, but habitat destruction for human development.

◻ RANDALL D. BABB, ARIZONA GAME AND FISH DEPARTMENT (2)

WESTERN BANDED GECKO
Coleonyx variegatus

DESCRIPTION: Narrow body; yellow-tan with darker bars or blotches above and pale below; skin appears soft and somewhat translucent, with pink hue to sides and limbs; large eyes rimmed with cream-colored movable lids; thin toes, no pads; tail thickens with fat storage; male has spurs at base of tail; often mistaken for baby Gila monster, but considerably smaller and lacking beaded skin
LENGTH: Up to 3 inches, plus tail of up to 3 inches
DIET: Insects and spiders
HABITAT: Desert scrub, dunes, grasslands and canyons
DISTRIBUTION: Most of Western and Southern Arizona
■ This is one of the more frequently encountered nocturnal reptiles in Arizona, especially around May, when males are out prowling for females. It doesn't look like other lizards — velvety skin, protuberant eyelids and dark, golden eyes, which are sometimes licked by a forkless tongue, make the gecko distinctive. This species lays two eggs per clutch and up to three clutches per year. Hatchlings emerge after an average of 45 days. Active hunting involves slow, cat-like advances and a quick twitch of the tail before grabbing the gecko's prey. The tail serves two more important roles: It stores fat and moisture, and it aids defense. When cornered, a banded gecko wiggles its tail, drawing the predator's attention to the wrong end. As the tail is grabbed, it detaches, allowing the gecko to make its escape. The tail eventually regrows, albeit shorter and with a mismatched pattern. Most lizards are silent, but if captured, this gecko chirps its distress.

LIVING WITH WILDLIFE

Never touch a desert tortoise in the wild. Its defense mechanism is to urinate, and since it doesn't drink much water, that moisture is precious — losing it puts the animal at risk of dehydration and death. If you must intervene because a tortoise is in immediate danger crossing a road, gently lift it (not too high) and carefully put it on the other side, facing the direction it was going.

Western banded gecko

TIGER WHIPTAIL

Aspidoscelis tigris

DESCRIPTION: Slender body; mottled gray to honey-brown; light spotting on sides; faint dorsal stripes; pointed snout; long and tapering tail; male has blackish throat and chest; juvenile has blue tail

LENGTH: 2.5 to 4.5 inches, plus tail of up to 6 inches

DIET: Insects (especially termites, cicadas and beetles), spiders, scorpions, some small lizards

HABITAT: Desert scrub, dunes, canyons, bajadas and hillsides

DISTRIBUTION: Most of Western and Southwestern Arizona; parts of north and southeast

■ This speedy lizard prefers open terrain where it can easily run from bush to bush. It is diurnal or sometimes crepuscular and spends most of its day actively foraging or digging for prey. Rarely does it climb. Being alert and quick afoot helps the whiptail avoid predators. But like many other lizards, it will sacrifice its tail if caught. Built-in fracture plates allow the tail to quickly detach — for show, the lost member continues to wriggle, distracting the attacker while the whiptail escapes. In time a new tail, a stumpier version of the original, will grow. Mating begins in spring, and females usually lay two to four eggs per year.

SIMILAR SPECIES: Arizona has 11 species of whiptail lizards, but the plateau whiptail (northern half of Arizona) is the only other wide-ranging species. It's brownish-black with six or seven cream stripes and a light-blue tail.

Tiger whiptail (male)

Common chuckwalla (male)

COMMON CHUCKWALLA

Sauromalus ater

DESCRIPTION: Wide-bellied; baggy and sandpaper-like skin; male is gray-black (often with reddish speckling) and tail is thick, blunt-ended and tan or yellowish (rarely orange); female is plain gray or faintly mottled or barred; juvenile is gray with yellow bands on body and tail; should not be confused with beady-skinned Gila monster
LENGTH: 5 to 9 inches, plus tail of 4 to 8 inches
DIET: Leaves, flowers and fruits; occasional insects
HABITAT: Rocky terrain within desert scrub; creosote bushes usually present
DISTRIBUTION: Western half of Arizona, scattered through Sonoran, Mohave and Great Basin deserts

■ The genus name *Sauromalus* means "flat lizard" — fitting for this large, diurnal reptile, often seen by hikers as it basks on trailside boulders. It is adapted for extreme desert temperatures, and only after sunbathing, warmed into animation, does it forage for food. If threatened, the chuckwalla scurries into a rock crevice and inflates its body, wedging itself in place. Breeding begins in May; males are territorial and mate with several females. Clutch size increases as a mother grows and can range from five to 16 eggs. Laid in a moist underground burrow, the eggs incubate for approximately 35 days. Like most lizards, hatchlings are precocial, left to survive on their own. Unless food is abundant, females may skip a year between broods.

Eastern collared lizard (male)

EASTERN COLLARED LIZARD
Crotaphytus collaris

DESCRIPTION: Sturdy body; blue-green with light spots and faint yellow bars; two black collars; large head (sometimes yellow); long and tapering tail; female more drab, with orange marks on neck and sides before egg-laying
LENGTH: 3 to 4.5 inches, plus tail of 5 to 9 inches; male larger than female
DIET: Small lizards, some snakes, insects, spiders, occasional plant matter
HABITAT: Desert scrub, grasslands, woodlands and canyons; prefers open, rocky areas
DISTRIBUTION: Eastern half and parts of West-Central Arizona, up to 8,000 feet
■ The eastern collared lizard is a fierce hunter with powerful jaws. It is even capable of sprinting upright — body at a 45-degree angle, front legs raised and tail lifted for balance. Perhaps because its tail is used so dynamically, the lizard is less likely to lose it during an escape. It's primarily carnivorous, and much of its day is spent in pursuit of prey, although it also enjoys basking in the sun. The male is territorial. After mating, a female buries up to 14 eggs (four to six on average), which hatch in summer or early fall. Babies are only about 1.5 inches long, excluding their tails. Hybridization with the Great Basin collared lizard has been described.
SIMILAR SPECIES: The Great Basin collared lizard (far-west and northwest deserts) and Sonoran collared lizard (southwest) are generally divided by the Gila River. Neither is as colorful as the eastern variety.

DESERT SPINY LIZARD
Sceloporus magister

DESCRIPTION: Thick body with keeled scales that are pointed and conspicuously overlapping; tan, gray or golden brown with variable spotting on back; yellow scales scattered on sides; black wedges on neck; head sometimes orange; male has teal on belly and throat
LENGTH: 3.5 to 5.5 inches, plus tale of up to 7 inches
DIET: Insects, some other invertebrates, small lizards, occasional plant matter
HABITAT: Desert scrub, grasslands and woodlands; sometimes in trees or atop logs, or near rock piles or packrat nests
DISTRIBUTION: Most of Arizona, except Mogollon Rim and parts of northeast
■ This diurnal reptile is often seen in male-female pairs. Although it's wary and quick to cover, using crevices and packrat nests for shelter, a patient

Desert spiny lizard (male)

 TOP: SUE TATTERSON ABOVE: RANDALL D. BABB, ARIZONA GAME AND FISH DEPARTMENT

Greater short-horned lizard

observer will find it compelling to watch. The male is aggressively territorial and engages in an array of eccentric behaviors during breeding season: head-bobbing, push-ups, dewlap displays, mouth-gaping and inflated posturing. After spring mating, a female lays three to 18 eggs. The lizard has a special adaptation called metachromatism — it can change color to help regulate body temperature. In cold weather, its skin turns dark to absorb warming rays of sunlight; in hot weather, its skin color becomes lighter and more reflective.

SIMILAR SPECIES: The Clark's spiny lizard (southeast and along the southern side of the Mogollon Rim) has drab, mottled coloring, often with a turquoise-blue tint.

GREATER SHORT-HORNED LIZARD
Phrynosoma hernandesi

DESCRIPTION: Body is flat, oval and spiked; horny plates on back of broad head have a center gap; splotchy pattern, cryptic coloration (usually copper, gray or tan); sides fringed with spiny scales; short, narrow tail
LENGTH: 2 to 5 inches, plus tail of 1 to 2 inches; female larger than male
DIET: Primarily ants; some beetles and other invertebrates

HABITAT: Forests, woodlands and arid grasslands from 4,000 to 11,000 feet; usually seen in sunny areas with sparse vegetation
DISTRIBUTION: Across most of Northern, Central and Southeastern Arizona

■ Despite the provocative nickname "horny toad," this is a lizard (toads are amphibians and don't have tails). Because the greater short-horned lizard is diurnal and terrestrial, often foraging out in the open, exceptional camouflage helps it hide in plain view. In fact, standing motionless is its most common defense. It can also squirt blood from its eyes to deter attacking predators — canids are said to be particularly repulsed. This species is cold tolerant. Unlike other horned lizards, it resides in high-elevation regions and instead of laying eggs, females give live birth. A brood of about 16 young is typically delivered after the March-to-May breeding season.

SIMILAR SPECIES: The desert horned lizard (west and south) has a bulbous head with paired horns at its nape, heavy mottling and a light dorsal stripe. The regal horned lizard (parts of south) is active year-round; it has no distinct pattern, but its middle dorsal is lighter than its sides. A few other, less common horned-lizard species also inhabit Arizona.

VENOMOUS

GILA MONSTER

Heloderma suspectum

DESCRIPTION: Large, stout body; beady skin is black and peach (or orange, pink or yellow); those in west and northwest characteristically have banded patterns, while those in central and southeast are usually reticulated; snout always black; short, thick tail; small, black eyes; dark, forked tongue
LENGTH: 9 to 14 inches, plus tail of 6 to 10 inches
DIET: Nestling mammals and birds (especially eggs), some reptiles, insects, carrion
HABITAT: Desert scrub (especially foothills and rocky bajadas) and woodlands
DISTRIBUTION: Most of Western, West-Central and Southern Arizona
VENOM: Potent neurotoxins but low yield; one component has been synthesized into a pharmaceutical drug for diabetic patients

■ This dazzling reptile, the only venomous lizard native to the United States, is protected by law. Old myths led to a fearsome reputation, but there have been no reported fatalities. Bites to humans, while painful, are rare because Gila monsters are never aggressive unless harassed.

📷 BILL LOVE

Gila monster

Too close? A hiss should be fair warning to back off, as this normally slow-moving lizard can strike fast when necessary. Its powerful, clamping jaws are lined with small, grooved teeth. Its venom (used primarily for defense) is not injected but, with a chewing action, is oozed into the bite wound from glands along the lower gum line. The chances of seeing a wild Gila monster are slim. It spends up to 98 percent of its life in subterranean burrows, so even though it's considered "active" from March to November, very little of that activity takes place above ground. It eats infrequently. Hindered by a lumbering gait, the Gila monster cannot capture quick-footed prey. Instead, it uses its acute sense of smell to ferret out bird and mammal nests, which it raids, gorging as much as possible and storing fat in its tail. Males sometimes wrestle for dominance during breeding season, and, like all lizards, mating involves the male and female connecting cloacas. The duration of the Gila monster's reproductive cycle is rather unusual: Mating takes place around May, and two to 12 (six on average) eggs are buried in July or August. Those eggs are believed to incubate through winter before hatching around the following May — making the whole process, from fertilization to offspring, a full year.

Western diamondback rattlesnake

RATTLESNAKES

Arizona has more rattlesnake species than any other state — 13 of them. These vipers (family *Viperidae*) possess needle-like fangs, which fold back when the mouth is closed. When erect, they can inject deadly venom for either predation or protection. Each species' venom has a unique chemical composition. Its level of danger is determined by the potency of toxins and volume injected (yield), which are described on the following pages. Rattlesnakes are recognized by their large, triangular heads and defined by tails with interlocking links of keratin (the same substance as our fingernails) that rattle when shaken (an average of 50 times per second). Each time a rattlesnake sheds its skin, another link is added. Since young, growing snakes shed more frequently than old snakes, more links are accumulated early in life. And because these links may break off, scientific measurements for length do not include the rattle. As with all serpents, a rattlesnake has a forked tongue that augments information collected through the nostrils.

Flicking out, the tines capture airborne chemicals, which are "smelled" by the Jacobson's organ at the back of the mouth. The nickname "pit viper" comes from small, heat-sensing holes (loreal pits) near the snakes' nostrils, which help detect warm prey. During the coldest months, rattlesnakes enter brumation, possibly with two or more sharing a winter den, rock crevice or dirt tunnel. Spring emergence marks the start of breeding season, a time when males compete for females (except sidewinders, which don't seem to fight among themselves). During mating, couples entwine their sinewy tails and the male everts his sex organ (hemipenis) to connect with the female's cloaca. Rattlesnakes are ovoviviparous, which means thin-membrane eggs incubate inside the mother's body. During the summer monsoon season, the female gives live birth, delivering a litter of one to 24 babies (four to six on average). Rattlesnakes face many predators, especially in their first year. Birds of prey, predatory mammals, roadrunners and kingsnakes will all take a meal if they can. Should a snake survive, its life span may be more than 20 years. Although fear-inducing, rattlesnakes typically are not aggressive to humans and rarely strike without escalating stages of defense. Less than 1 percent of bites in Arizona result in human death.

LIVING WITH WILDLIFE

If you hear a rattle while hiking, freeze. Calmly scan the ground until the snake is located, and slowly move in the opposite direction. Given the snake's poor vision, don't be alarmed if it unwittingly slithers toward you; just keep backing away. All rattlesnake bites are potentially deadly and require immediate medical attention.

VENOMOUS
WESTERN DIAMONDBACK RATTLESNAKE
Crotalus atrox

DESCRIPTION: Heavy-bodied; tan-gray, peppered with large brown diamonds on back; two light diagonal stripes on face touch upper lip; tail ringed with broad black-and-white bands of approximately equal width
LENGTH: Up to 5 feet (Arizona's largest rattlesnake)
DIET: Rodents, rabbits, birds and some lizards

HABITAT: Desert scrub, grasslands, woodlands, hillsides, bajadas and urban areas; likes packrat nests
DISTRIBUTION: More than half the state, especially the southwest
VENOM: Responsible for the majority of rattlesnake bites and related deaths in Arizona; potent hemotoxins and high yield cause severe hemorrhaging and tissue damage
■ The Western diamondback — known to hold ground and defend itself if antagonized — gained national attention in 1995, when baseball fans voted to name an emergent major-league team the Arizona Diamondbacks.

Mohave rattlesnake

DIET: Small mammals, some birds, lizards, frogs and toads
HABITAT: Flat desert scrub, low bajadas and grasslands
DISTRIBUTION: Most of Western and Southern Arizona
VENOM: Considered Arizona's most toxic rattlesnake; composition of venom varies, but uniquely potent neurotoxins and high yield are life-threatening
■ The Mohave rattlesnake is not a strong climber, so it tends to stay in areas of level terrain.

VENOMOUS
RIDGE-NOSED RATTLESNAKE
Crotalus willardi

DESCRIPTION: Reddish tan-brown, with thin, buff cross bars and bold brown and white facial markings; nose slopes up to a ridged tip
LENGTH: 1.5 to 2 feet
DIET: Young eat lizards and centipedes; adults eat small mammals, lizards and birds
HABITAT: Wooded canyons near water
DISTRIBUTION: Santa Rita, Whetstone,

VENOMOUS
MOHAVE RATTLESNAKE
Crotalus scutulatus

DESCRIPTION: Greenish gray-brown with crisp, dark diamonds; may appear similar to diamondback, but several traits distinguish: dorsal blotches have uniformly colored centers, rear facial stripe sweeps back away from lip, and black tail rings are narrower than white
LENGTH: 3 feet (average)

Ridge-nosed rattlesnake

Sidewinder

Huachuca and Patagonia mountains of South-Central Arizona

VENOM: Comparatively weak toxicity, low yield

■ This species was first identified in Arizona in 1900 and chosen as the state reptile in 1986. It has excellent camouflage, readily blending in with canyon leaf litter. A rare natural hybridization with the banded rock rattlesnake (*Crotalus lepidus*) has been described.

SIMILAR SPECIES: The New Mexico ridge-nosed rattlesnake (Peloncillo Mountains of extreme Southeastern Arizona) is a threatened subspecies that lacks distinct facial marks. All ridge-nosed rattlesnakes are protected.

VENOMOUS

SIDEWINDER

Crotalus cerastes

DESCRIPTION: Rough, bumpy scales; pinkish to creamy tan, with darker dorsal blotches with white between; each eye has brown stripe behind and distinctive "horn" above

LENGTH: Up to 2 feet

DIET: Lizards, rodents (especially kangaroo rats), some birds

HABITAT: Desert scrub and dunes; prefers open, sandy terrain

DISTRIBUTION: Southwest Sonoran and northwest Mohave deserts

VENOM: Relatively low toxicity and yield

■ Sidewinders are symbolic of old Western films, characterized as camouflaged coils of death. In truth, they are less dangerous to humans than many other rattlesnake species. Adapted for life in the hottest regions of Arizona, these chiefly nocturnal serpents take cover from the summer sun. When not occupying underground burrows, they may be discovered curled in meager patches of shade or partially buried in the sand. J-shaped tracks are the markings of their unique sideways locomotion, which, with rapid propulsion, requires minimal contact with scorching sand — the snake version of tiptoeing.

Sonoran coralsnake

VENOMOUS

SONORAN CORALSNAKE

Micruroides euryxanthus

DESCRIPTION: Uniformly narrow with little tapering; glossy scales; wide bands of black, red and cream (or yellow) encircling the body; blunt, black face; small, black eyes
LENGTH: 1 to 2 feet
DIET: Small snakes and occasionally lizards
HABITAT: Desert scrub (especially rocky canyons, bajadas and washes), grasslands and woodlands
DISTRIBUTION: Most of Southern Arizona
VENOM: Potent neurotoxins, but comparatively low yield due to small size of snake

■ Coralsnakes are quite secretive, so despite decent distribution in the lower half of the state, they are rarely encountered. That makes them a real treat to see. Primarily nocturnal, they are occasionally spotted on overcast days. Their aposematic coloring deters predators, which may be one of the reasons they are not antagonistic by nature. Although a coralsnake is more likely to hide its head in its coils and present its tail than to bite, remember that it is venomous and should never be touched. Another defense strategy involves noisily popping gas from its cloaca. Coralsnakes are not in the same family as rattlesnakes; their fangs are shorter and fixed in place, there are no heat-sensing facial pits, and they don't give live birth. Eggs (two or three) are laid each summer, underground or in a crevice. It is in such dark, earthy places that coralsnakes spend much of their time.
SIMILAR SPECIES: The Sonoran mountain kingsnake (see opposite page) has a light-colored snout. The milksnake (parts of northeast)

RANDALL D. BABB, ARIZONA GAME AND FISH DEPARTMENT (2)

■ Arizona's other kingsnakes, the common kingsnakes, come in a lot of color variations. The majority are banded black and cream. Some are just black. Others are patchy brown and yellow. But the Sonoran mountain kingsnake's color is exceptional. The vivid red bands are not only eye-catching but an example of mimicry — in this case, they mimic the aposematic coloring of the venomous Sonoran coralsnake. With kingsnakes, death does not occur by venom but by constriction: Prey is squeezed until suffocated. Sonoran mountain kingsnakes hunt during the day, normally at ground level, but they can also climb when necessary. While common kingsnakes are known to eat rattlesnakes and are immune to their venom, that behavior has not been documented in this smaller species. Generally regarded as docile with humans, they may hiss and strike if threatened or emit a pungent musk. Females lay two to nine eggs in summer, and hatchlings take three to four years to reach maturity.

SIMILAR SPECIES: The milksnake (parts of northeast) has a black face. Among other Arizona kingsnakes, the California kingsnake (most common species, nearly statewide) has black and cream bands; the desert kingsnake (far southeast) is speckled yellow with black-brown blotches; and the Western black kingsnake (southeastern edge) is monochromatic.

has a black face but a longer, tapered tail. Both are non-venomous and have red and yellow bands separated by black.

SONORAN MOUNTAIN KINGSNAKE
Lampropeltis pyromelana

DESCRIPTION: Medium-thick body tapers toward tail; unevenly spaced red, black and cream (sometimes yellowish) bands; narrower banding and light-colored snout distinguish it from coralsnake
LENGTH: 1.5 to 3.5 feet
DIET: Lizards, rodents, birds and bats
HABITAT: Mountain forests, wooded canyons, rock piles and talus slopes, often near streams or springs
DISTRIBUTION: Northwest through central and Mogollon Rim to southeast

Sonoran mountain kingsnake

Gophersnake

GOPHERSNAKE
Pituophis catenifer

DESCRIPTION: Thick, muscular body; dorsal scales are keeled and appear bumpy; tan-yellow with brown (sometimes blackish or reddish) blotches; frequently mistaken for rattlesnake, but head more narrow, pupils round and no rattle on tail
LENGTH: Up to 7.5 feet (Arizona's longest snake)
DIET: Small mammals, birds, bird eggs (nest raider), some snakes and lizards
HABITAT: Desert scrub, grasslands, woodlands, forests and agricultural areas
DISTRIBUTION: Statewide
■ This widespread Arizona snake is frequently seen on trails and roads during the temperate days of spring and fall. A strong climber, it may also be found in trees. As summer heats up, it becomes more nocturnal. Like the Sonoran mountain kingsnake, the gophersnake is a mimic — not in color, but in behavior. When threatened, it does a fair impersonation of a rattlesnake by raising and flattening its head, puffing up and hissing — it even vibrates the tip of its tail to rattle the leaf litter. Despite this intimidating display, it is not venomous. It kills it prey by constriction and can ingest a larger-than-expected meal, expanding its jaws and throat to surprising proportions. While it hunts, it too is hunted. Many predators, especially raptors, eat gophersnakes. Successful reproduction helps keep populations stable. In spring, males energetically compete to mate. The eggs that a female lays in June and July (two to 24 of them) are left unguarded to hatch in August. Like most snakes in the region, this species brumates through winter.
SIMILAR SPECIES: The glossy snake (statewide, except highest elevations) is smaller (up to 4 feet) with smooth dorsal scales.

TERRESTRIAL GARTERSNAKE
Thamnophis elegans

DESCRIPTION: Brown to olive-gray above, with one cream dorsal stripe and irregular black spots; may also have pale side stripes or lack stripes entirely
LENGTH: Up to 3 feet
DIET: Amphibians, invertebrates (including worms, snails and insects), rodents, small birds and fish
HABITAT: Grasslands and forests, often near lakes and riparian areas; from 4,800 to 9,000 feet
DISTRIBUTION: Most of Northern and Northeastern Arizona
■ The terrestrial gartersnake's name belies this serpent's strength as a swimmer. Although

Terrestrial gartersnake

Coachwhip

most of its diurnal life is spent on land, it prefers to have riparian habitat nearby and often hunts in water. This gartersnake may employ a constricting strategy to subdue prey. And while it is not officially listed as venomous, its saliva has unique myotoxic enzymes to help break down muscle tissues. It is also ovoviviparous; mothers give live birth between July and September. Although reports of brood size vary, it probably averages about eight offspring a year.

SIMILAR SPECIES: The black-necked gartersnake (central and southeast) is olive gray with a bright-yellow dorsal stripe, a solid gray head and black patches on either side of its neck.

COACHWHIP
Masticophis (Coluber) flagellum

DESCRIPTION: Extremely long and slender body; many color variations, from dark brown to rose, gray or tan; sometimes barred; smooth scales have braided appearance, especially on tail (resembles a whip); large eyes with round pupils

LENGTH: 3 to 6 feet
DIET: Lizards, snakes (including rattlesnakes), mammals (rodents and bats), small birds and some amphibians
HABITAT: Desert scrub, woodlands, grasslands and agricultural areas; generally avoids dense vegetation
DISTRIBUTION: South, west-central and northwest

■ This is a common snake, but known for grace and speed, it often slips from sight before it can be recognized. To escape predators, such as coyotes and raptors, it even may climb trees or cactuses. Like all snakes, the coachwhip is carnivorous. But unlike most snakes, relatively strong vision aids hunting, and it sometimes travels with its head raised to get a look around. Despite myths, it does not chase humans. As a rule, its first defense is to race for cover, but it may repeatedly bite if captured. Mating takes place from April to July. Sometime thereafter, up to 24 eggs are laid inside a mammal burrow. Each egg is 1 to 1.5 inches long, and incubation is 76 to 79 days.

Arizona treefrog

AMPHIBIANS AND FISH

📷 COREY ANDERSON

TOADS AND FROGS

Toads *are* frogs. Frogs make up the amphibian order *Anura*, while toads make up the anuran family *Bufonidae*, generally characterized as having more terrestrial habits, shorter legs and drier, warty skin. Male bufonids also possess a latent ovary, called a Bidder's organ, that may become active if their testes are damaged or non-functioning. There are 24 native species of anurans in Arizona. They have excellent hearing (the flat disc behind the eye is an external eardrum) and a sticky tongue for catching prey. Their life cycle is complex. In the breeding season, males call out to attract females, amplifying the sound by inflating and deflating balloon-like vocal sacs, usually located under the chin. Each species has a distinct call. During mating, the male (generally smaller in size) clings to the female and fertilizes her eggs as she deposits them in water. The eggs hatch tadpoles, aquatic larvae that have internal gills for breathing in water and tails for paddling. Algae, detritus and plankton form the typical tadpole diet. In time, tadpoles metamorphose — they grow legs, develop lungs and lose their tails — and become adult frogs that can inhabit both land and water. Anurans, like all amphibians, produce protective skin secretions (some more irritating than others), and certain species have parotoid glands with potent toxins. Still, mortality is high, as they are preyed upon by many animals, including raccoons, birds, snakes and occasionally each other. Because absorbent skin makes them especially susceptible to damaging chemicals and contaminants in their habitats, frogs serve as indicators of ecosystem health, and efforts to clean up and preserve their wetlands benefit all dependent life.

SONORAN DESERT TOAD
Incilius alvarius

DESCRIPTION: Fairly smooth skin, olive with small yellow-brown spots; kidney-shaped parotoid glands; distinctive white warts at corners of mouth
LENGTH: 4 to 7.5 inches (Arizona's largest toad)
DIET: Opportunistic carnivore; insects, arachnids, snails, lizards, mice, other amphibians
HABITAT: Desert scrub, streams, pools, stock tanks, riparian grasslands and woodlands; up to 5,700 feet
DISTRIBUTION: Most of Southern Arizona
CALL: Weak, low-pitched croak that lasts about a second
■ This bufonid — also called the Colorado River toad — can secrete a milky poison. It is nocturnal and most active during summer rains. Breeding in desert locales may be a one-night event, and males sometimes forego calling to simply search out females. Up to 8,000 eggs are laid in a gelatinous string, and tadpoles metamorphose in six to 10 weeks. Daytime and winters are commonly spent underground.

LIVING WITH WILDLIFE

The Sonoran Desert toad's defensive skin secretions are toxic enough to make a full-grown dog extremely sick (although death is rare). Early symptoms of exposure are excessive drooling, a staggering gait and pawing at the mouth. Flush the dog's mouth with water and seek immediate veterinary attention.

Sonoran desert toad

SONORAN GREEN TOAD
Anaxyrus retiformis

DESCRIPTION: Vivid, reticulated pattern of green-yellow and black; white belly; large, oval-shaped parotoid glands

LENGTH: 1.5 to 2.5 inches

DIET: Small invertebrates (including termites)

HABITAT: Mainly valleys, low bajadas, ditches, washes and stock tanks; from 500 to 3,000 feet

DISTRIBUTION: South-Central Arizona to Mexico

CALL: Between a buzz and a whistle, lasting one to three seconds

■ This brightly colored toad is a favorite among herpetologists — for both its bold appearance and the fact that it is endemic to the Sonoran Desert. It emerges from subterranean dormancy in July and August, and breeding aggregations may reach 200 individuals. Eggs, laid singly or in clusters, hatch in two to three days, and pea-sized tadpoles develop into toadlets within two to three weeks.

SIMILAR SPECIES: The green toad (extreme Southeastern Arizona) is spotted, not reticulated.

Sonoran green toad

Woodhouse's toad

WOODHOUSE'S TOAD
Anaxyrus woodhousii

DESCRIPTION: Warty and yellow-brown skin, darker and blotchy on top, often with a whitish strip down the back; elongated parotoid glands
LENGTH: 2 to 5 inches
DIET: Insects (including larvae) and arachnids
HABITAT: Sandy wetlands, lakes, canals and stock tanks; sometimes urban areas
DISTRIBUTION: Most of Arizona
CALL: Like a loudly bleating sheep, lasting two to three seconds
■ This toad's breeding season is February to June (June to September in temporary ponds), and females can lay an astonishing 28,000 eggs. Tadpoles hatch in about eight weeks and have fully metamorphosed five to eight weeks later. In Arizona, the Woodhouse's toad has been seen mating with other toad species, and hybrids have been documented.

MEXICAN SPADEFOOT
Spea multiplicata

DESCRIPTION: Brownish-gray skin with dark blotches and red bumps; sharp black "spade" inside each hind foot; large, copper-colored eyes (pupils change from round to cat-like in bright light)
LENGTH: 1.5 to 2.5 inches

DIET: Invertebrates
HABITAT: Desert scrub, grasslands, woodlands and agricultural areas
DISTRIBUTION: Most of Eastern and Central Arizona
CALL: Long, slow trill
■ The Mexican spadefoot uses its horny spade for burrowing underground, where it remains inactive most of the year. It emerges during the summer monsoon season. Breeding takes place in temporary rain ponds. Some spadefoot tadpoles are omnivorous, while others are carnivorous, dining heavily on fairy shrimp. The carnivore tadpoles grow bigger jaws and become cannibalistic. Interestingly, the skin secretion of this species smells like peanuts.
SIMILAR SPECIES: Couch's spadefoot (south), Great Basin spadefoot (far northwest) and Plains spadefoot (northeast and southeast).

Mexican spadefoot

 TOP: PEGGY COLEMAN ABOVE: RANDALL D. BABB, ARIZONA GAME AND FISH DEPARTMENT

Arizona treefrog

ARIZONA TREEFROG

Hyla wrightorum

DESCRIPTION: Green to bronze on top; white belly; dark stripe through eye and down side (may break into spots); may have dark dorsal blotches; large, round toe pads (also on canyon treefrog) are distinctive
LENGTH: 2 inches (average)
DIET: Small invertebrates (especially insects, worms and spiders)
HABITAT: Stream banks, cienegas, ditches and stock tanks; above 5,000 feet
DISTRIBUTION: Mogollon Rim from Williams southeast into New Mexico

CALL: Series of short clacks

■ Schoolchildren selected the Arizona treefrog as the official state amphibian; it was designated in 1986. Like so many frogs in the Southwest, breeding takes place during summer monsoons. It tends to utilize temporary waters where there are fewer aquatic predators, and the male's chorus lasts only two to three days. Egg clusters are attached to vegetation, and emerging tadpoles metamorphose in 45 to 75 days. This species' back feet are only slightly webbed, and in its offseason, it is alleged to be arboreal.

CANYON TREEFROG
Hyla arenicolor

DESCRIPTION: Somewhat toad-like; warty skin with variable pattern; cryptic coloration for camouflage (usually gray, olive, pink or tan); yellow inside hind legs; large adhesive discs at toe tips
LENGTH: 1 to 2 inches
DIET: Algae and detritus for tadpoles; invertebrates for adults
HABITAT: Woodlands, canyons and riparian areas; usually among streamside boulders
DISTRIBUTION: Throughout state, except arid western deserts (Mohave, Sonoran)
CALL: Explosive, rattling whir

■ Finding a canyon treefrog can be challenging because of its tendency to hide in rock crevices. More significantly, it can change its coloring to match the stone. It is, in fact, such a master of camouflage that even attached to the open face of a boulder, it manages to vanish before the eyes. Crepuscular or nocturnal, it naturally makes its way to the water's edge to begin foraging at dusk. Breeding takes place in rain-filled streams, where a mere 100 or so eggs are laid by each adult female. Her eggs normally hatch within two weeks. Tadpoles become froglets in 45 to 75 days, except for those that hatch late in the season; they may overwinter, completing their metamorphosis the following spring. The canyon treefrog's skin secretion includes a mild irritant (as does the Arizona treefrog's).

Chiricahua leopard frog

CHIRICAHUA LEOPARD FROG
Lithobates chiricahuensis

DESCRIPTION: Stocky body; green or brown, with dark spots and skin folds running down each side of the back; upturned golden eyes
LENGTH: Less than 4.3 inches
DIET: Invertebrates (especially beetles, true bugs and flies), small vertebrates
HABITAT: Stock tanks, streams, cienegas and pools
DISTRIBUTION: Reduced to a fraction of historical range; distinct populations divided between the Mogollon Rim forests of East-Central Arizona and the semi-desert grasslands of Southeastern Arizona
CALL: Described as a "snore" lasting one to three seconds
CONSERVATION STATUS: Threatened

Canyon treefrog

TOP: CHRISTINA M. AKINS, ARIZONA GAME AND FISH DEPARTMENT
ABOVE: RANDALL D. BABB, ARIZONA GAME AND FISH DEPARTMENT

Arizona tiger salamander

ARIZONA TIGER SALAMANDER
Ambystoma mavortium nebulosum

DESCRIPTION: Thick-bodied; gray-brown with black or yellowish blotches; tiny, bulging eyes; rounded snout; larvae and lungless adults are olive-gray, with six protruding gills at neck; salamanders do not have ear holes or claws like lizards

LENGTH: 3 to 6.5 inches (head and body), plus tail of up to 7 inches

DIET: Mostly invertebrates; cannibalism in some larvae and gilled adults

HABITAT: Forested wetlands, ponds, lakes and stock tanks

DISTRIBUTION: Colorado Plateau and Mogollon Rim, Northeastern Arizona

■ These animals are best seen at night, particularly during heavy rains. Like other amphibians, Arizona tiger salamanders go through a complex physical transformation. Eggs hatch into legless larvae that soon grow limbs. Most adults lose their gills and move from an aquatic to a terrestrial lifestyle. In winter and spring, adults return to their natal ponds for breeding. Each female lays 200 to 2,000 eggs, which hatch about three weeks later. Tiger salamanders are splendid animals but can carry an infectious fungal disease called chytridiomycosis, which is deadly to some other amphibians. For that reason, salamanders should never be moved from one body of water to another.

SIMILAR SPECIES: Other subspecies include the endangered Sonoran tiger salamander (San Rafael Valley in southeast) and the introduced barred tiger salamander (south).

■ The Chiricahua leopard frog once was widespread in Arizona but is disappearing under the pressures of non-native predators (especially crawfish, bullfrogs and fish), a fungal disease (chytridiomycosis) and loss of habitat. Biologists are working to increase populations through habitat management and reintroduction of captive-bred frogs. Breeding season varies by elevation, but the Chiricahua leopard frog is primarily aquatic and requires calm, permanent water to successfully reproduce. Spherical egg masses (300 to 1,500 eggs) attached to submerged vegetation hatch in one to two weeks. Tadpoles take three to nine months to metamorphose, depending on whether they overwinter, as this species is inactive from November to February.

SIMILAR SPECIES: The northern leopard frog (north), Plains leopard frog (extreme southeast), lowland leopard frog (central and southeast) and relict leopard frog (northwest) tend to be smaller and have fewer spots.

Apache trout

FISH

Arizona used to have 36 native fish species, but one is already extirpated. Others are dwindling. Conservation teams are working to keep populations stable, but the challenge is twofold. Because water sources are now heavily managed and restricted, the state's aquatic landscape is not what it historically has been. Many natural habitats are disappearing. In addition, most of the fish species found in lakes and streams are non-native and were introduced for recreational purposes, and they prey on (or create tough competition for) local fish. The native species that remain are worth looking for, as they are varied in appearance and have some remarkable characteristics. Reproductive behavior varies. Most of them spawn in spring, when females either dig nests (like the Apache trout, desert sucker and longfin dace) or scatter their eggs randomly for fertilization (like the roundtail chub and desert pupfish). Fry generally emerge within a few days and reach maturity two or three years later.

APACHE TROUT
Oncorhynchus apache

DESCRIPTION: Golden yellow, with olive above and dark spots; white tip on dorsal fin; black line through eye
LENGTH: About 6 inches in streams; about 18 inches in lakes
DIET: Mainly aquatic insects
HABITAT: Mountain lakes and headwater streams
DISTRIBUTION: East-Central Arizona in the White Mountains
CONSERVATION STATUS: Threatened
■ The Apache trout became Arizona's state fish in 1986. It is endemic to Arizona and one of only two trout species native to the state (the other is the Gila trout). Its eggs take a lengthy 30 days to hatch.

DESERT SUCKER
Catostomus clarki

DESCRIPTION: Elongated body; green-brown coloring (may appear mottled); white-yellow belly; sucker-like mouth; in some populations, breeding adults develop orange-red stripe on side
LENGTH: 4 to 12 inches
DIET: Young primarily feed on aquatic insect larvae; adults use cartilage ridge on lower lip to scrape algae
HABITAT: Small to medium rivers, riffle streams and associated pools
DISTRIBUTION: Colorado River below Grand Canyon, Virgin River Basin, Gila River and tributaries
■ The desert sucker is still found throughout most of its historical range.

Desert sucker

Longfin dace

LONGFIN DACE
Agosia chrysogaster

DESCRIPTION: Silver and spindle-shaped body; dark lateral lines; one black spot at base of tail fin; sometimes gold flecks on sides; breeding male may turn brassy at base of fins and ventral surfaces
LENGTH: 2.5 inches
DIET: Opportunistically omnivorous; aquatic plants and invertebrates
HABITAT: Shallow streams with sandy bottoms
DISTRIBUTION: West-Central to Southeastern Arizona
■ This amazing minnow species has been reported to survive dry seasons beneath mats of moist filamentous algae and then reproduce within days of a rejuvenating rain.

ROUNDTAIL CHUB
Gila robusta

DESCRIPTION: Somewhat trout-like in shape; olive to silver above; white belly; breeding male develops red-orange color on ventral sides
LENGTH: 8 to 19 inches
DIET: Aquatic and land-based invertebrates

Roundtail chub

(including crawfish) and algae
HABITAT: Pools and eddies of medium-large rivers; prefers overhanging cliffs and/or vegetation
DISTRIBUTION: Tributaries of the Little Colorado, Bill Williams and Gila rivers
■ The roundtail chub is still common in certain rivers, although its overall numbers appear to be in considerable decline.

HUMPBACK CHUB
Gila cypha

DESCRIPTION: Silvery and streamlined body with fleshy hump behind head; large fins; sharply forked tail; breeding adults develop bumps (tubercles) and may have orange-red fins and cheeks
LENGTH: Less than 20 inches
DIET: Mainly aquatic invertebrates; some fish

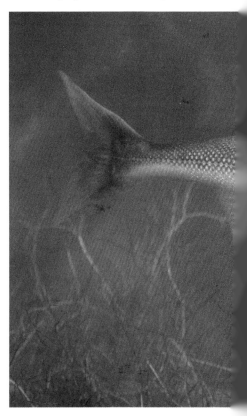

and algae

HABITAT: Large rivers (including fast-running currents, deep and turbulent waters, calmer pools, backwaters and eddies)

DISTRIBUTION: Colorado and Little Colorado rivers (largest population in Grand Canyon National Park)

CONSERVATION STATUS: Endangered

■ A humpback chub may live as long as 30 years.

Desert pupfish

DESERT PUPFISH
Cyprinodon macularius

DESCRIPTION: Squat-bodied; tan-olive with darker vertical bars; breeding male turns blue with yellow fins and tail

LENGTH: 2 to 3 inches; male larger than female

DIET: Aquatic invertebrates, algae and detritus

HABITAT: Shallow, warm waters, including cienegas, desert springs and salty marshes; below 5,000 feet

DISTRIBUTION: Central to Southern Arizona

CONSERVATION STATUS: Endangered

■ The male desert pupfish is aggressively territorial, especially during breeding season. This species may reach maturity as early as six weeks, and its life span is only a year or two.

SIMILAR SPECIES: The Sonoyta pupfish is found only at Quitobaquito Springs in Southern Arizona and in one river in Mexico.

Humpback chub

📷 MOCHELLE PADGETT

Wildlife Viewing Areas

Wild animals inhabit every niche of Arizona. They ramble, flutter, slither and hop across barren desert floors and snowy mountain crests, grass-lined country roads and hushed urban streets. They soar high as the heavens and root in earthy tunnels, moist and cool. Day and night, winter and summer — always, they are there. And yet, when you go exploring in the outdoors, even in a designated wildlife viewing area, there's never a guarantee that you'll see any wild animals at all. That's what makes the search so compelling. Spotting a bobcat slinking beneath a rocky outcrop, a golden eagle carving the clouds, a misty-eyed deer grazing among the pines or a flashy lizard doing push-ups on a sunlit rock is like a finding a little nugget of gold. It makes you hungry to find more.

With inquisitive patience, you will.

Odds are, the more time you spend looking, the more wildlife you'll see. Add a road trip to your search, and you have the makings of an adventure, a treasure hunt — one that deserves a good camera and a like-minded companion. There are many bountiful places throughout Arizona to seek wildlife and several books and online resources to help you find notable hiking trails where animals might be

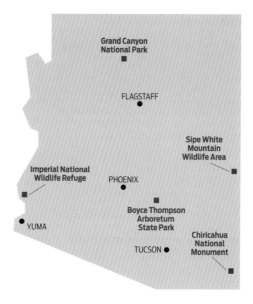

Grand Canyon National Park

FLAGSTAFF

Sipe White Mountain Wildlife Area

Imperial National Wildlife Refuge

PHOENIX

Boyce Thompson Arboretum State Park

YUMA

Chiricahua National Monument

TUCSON

Rock squirrel, South Rim, Grand Canyon National Park

observed. On the following pages are five of the best locations from around the state — something within driving distance for every resident or visitor, a broad selection of topography, and the chance to experience different systems of state and national land preservation — along with tips to help you spot more animals while you're out there. Before you hit the road, be sure to check for seasonal closures and visitor hours.

Of course, you needn't go anywhere at all. The closest wildlife viewing area is your own backyard. Pull out a chair and watch the birds and lizards and insects go about their day. They're more beautiful than you remember. More fascinating, too.

No matter where your quest takes you, try to enjoy each wildlife sighting to its fullest. Stop. Breathe. Listen. Look. Relish the moment and celebrate creation. You will find no better way to rejuvenate your own spirit than to quietly connect with nature in all its wonder.

NORTHERN ARIZONA

GRAND CANYON NATIONAL PARK
Grand Canyon

A hike into this colorful chasm promises dynamic shifts of habitat. Descend from towering pine forests, through piñon-juniper woodlands and desert scrub, to the lush riparian corridor of the Colorado River. Of Arizona's three national parks, the Grand Canyon is by far the most biologically diverse, supporting an array of animals that includes more than 350 bird species and 89 mammals. At the popular South Rim, some of the wildlife — birds, squirrels, even deer — have become habituated to humans and will casually cross the main trails. Keep an eye out for California condors floating beyond the Canyon ledge. Across the gorge, the 8,000-foot North Rim is far more rugged and remote; closed for winter, it receives just 10 percent of the park's visitors. Meander through quiet, green stands with Kaibab squirrels scampering around vanilla-scented ponderosas or breezy meadows where mule deer and (non-native) bison graze. If driving to the North Rim, consider a quick stop at the Vermilion Cliffs condor-release site (off U.S.

Bighorns, Hermit Trail, Grand Canyon National Park

Route 89A at Bureau of Land Management Road 1065; follow the dirt road to the marked and shaded viewing area). Look for whitewash high on the red cliffs — that's where the condors roost.
ESTABLISHED: 1919
SIZE: 1.2 million acres
ELEVATION: 2,200 to 8,800 feet (South Rim is 6,800 feet)
HABITAT: From highest to lowest elevation: forest, woodland, desert scrub, riparian
WILDLIFE INCLUDES: Elk, mule deer, pronghorns, cougars, foxes, river otters, raccoons, ringtails, porcupines, Arizona myotis, beavers, Abert's (and Kaibab) squirrels, cliff chipmunks, Ord's kangaroo rats, California condors, eagles, owls, peregrine falcons, woodpeckers, hummingbirds, Merriam's turkeys, mountain bluebirds, swallows, phoebes, Western tanagers, water birds, desert tortoises, Gila monsters, chuckwallas, banded geckos, Arizona tiger salamanders, Arizona and Canyon treefrogs, humpback chubs, scorpions, butterflies
DIRECTIONS: To reach the South Rim from Flagstaff, go west on Interstate 40 to Williams, then north on State Route 64. To reach the North Rim from Flagstaff, go north on U.S. Route 89, then west on U.S. Route 89A and south on State Route 67.
ENTRY FEE: Yes
TRAILS: Many miles of trails at all elevations and difficulty levels

SERVICES AND FACILITIES: Visitors centers, restrooms, food, museums, exhibits, presentations, hotels, campgrounds, interpretive signs, bicycle rentals, gift shops
MORE INFORMATION: 928-638-7888 or www.nps.gov/grca

SIPE WHITE MOUNTAIN WILDLIFE AREA
Eagar

The emerald-and-gold highlands of Eastern Arizona sustain many montane species, including the elusive Mexican gray wolf. Currently, there are 27 wildlife areas in Arizona, and all are worth exploring. But while most have limited, if any, services or facilities, the Sipe White Mountain Wildlife Area hosts guests at a lovely visitors center along the greenbelt of Rudd Creek. Birds flit around the orchard.

Summer beavers dam the rippling stream, and amphibians chirp from the dewy wetlands. Hike up amid bushy piñon pines, where wild turkeys are known to roam, and enjoy a stunning view of Escudilla Mountain pushing skyward to 10,912 feet. Or take an amble across high-elevation meadows, stretches of amber grass that conceal Montezuma quail and draw graceful herds of elk and pronghorns. For archaeology enthusiasts, the property also safeguards petroglyphs and the remains of an Ancestral Puebloan village. Nearby, Terry Flat Loop (farther south on U.S. routes 180 and 191, east on Forest Road 56, then 5 miles to the loop fork) offers a scenic drive or hike around Escudilla Mountain. Although the area was badly damaged during the Wallow Fire in 2011, new tree growth is revitalizing habitat for wildlife.
PURCHASED: 1993
SIZE: 1,362 acres
ELEVATION: 7,625 to 7,836 feet

Sipe White Mountain Wildlife Area

HABITAT: Forests, woodlands, grasslands, riparian areas, wetlands

WILDLIFE INCLUDES: Elk, mule deer, pronghorns, cougars, Mexican gray wolves, gray foxes, coyotes, beavers, badgers, jackrabbits, Abert's squirrels, ground squirrels, bald eagles, hawks, peregrine falcons, kestrels, Merriam's turkeys, Montezuma quail, acorn woodpeckers, Steller's jays, mountain bluebirds, white-breasted nuthatches, robins, broad-tailed hummingbirds, widgeons, buffleheads, herons, killdeer, Eastern collared and greater short-horned lizards, Chiricahuan leopard frogs, Arizona treefrogs, Apache trout

DIRECTIONS: From Eagar, go south on U.S. routes 180 and 191, and watch for the marked turnoff between mileposts 404 and 405. Turn right (west) and follow the improved dirt road for 5 miles.

ENTRY FEE: No

TRAILS: Rudd Creek Loop (2.5 miles, easy), Homestead (1.5 miles, easy), High Point (1 mile, moderate), Trinity (350 yards, wheelchair accessible)

SERVICES AND FACILITIES: Visitors center (seasonal), restrooms, water, workshops, interpretive signs, spotting scope, trail benches, picnic area

MORE INFORMATION: 928-367-4281 or http://azgfdportal.az.gov/wildlife/viewing/wheretogo/sipe

CENTRAL ARIZONA
BOYCE THOMPSON ARBORETUM STATE PARK
Superior

Nestled at the foot of Picketpost Mountain is a true desert paradise, replete with scenic vistas, leafy-green foliage and glimmering water. It's no wonder that millionaire William Boyce Thompson purchased this treasured land and felt compelled to preserve it as the state's first arboretum. Now, it's the state's largest botanical garden and one of 29 Arizona state parks. Sun and shade dapple the footpaths that wander between drought-resistant plants, including strange and beautiful flora from around the globe. Spring butterflies linger on blossoms. Lizards scuttle in the undergrowth. At Ayer Lake,

Turkey vultures, Boyce Thompson Arboretum State Park

Imperial National Wildlife Refuge

native water birds wade among the cattails, with migratory species — genuine snowbirds — joining the delegation each winter. Just beyond, the main trail loops into an open canyon, where ground squirrels peek from lofty boulders and birdsong echoes off the cactus-strewn slopes, spilling into the plush cottonwoods along Queen Creek. The creek's verdant banks are ideal for wildlife, so allow ample time to peek around that area. With more than 250 avian species recorded within its boundaries, Boyce Thompson Arboretum State Park is listed as an Important Birding Area by the National Audubon Society.

ESTABLISHED: 1924 (arboretum), 1976 (state park)

SIZE: 392 acres

ELEVATION: 2,400 feet (approximate)

HABITAT: Desert scrub, canyon, riparian areas, wetlands

WILDLIFE INCLUDES: Mule deer, javelinas, bobcats, gray foxes, coatis, raccoons, cottontails, ground squirrels, cliff chipmunks, golden eagles, hawks, turkey vultures, peregrine falcons, ravens, great horned owls, wild turkeys, Gambel's quail, doves, northern mockingbirds, curve-billed thrashers, northern cardinals, swallows, brown-headed cowbirds, gilded flickers, Gila woodpeckers, red-naped sapsuckers, phainopeplas, red-winged blackbirds, white-breasted nuthatches, wrens, black phoebes, hummingbirds, verdins, house finches, water birds, Gila monsters, lizards, coachwhips, gophersnakes, gartersnakes, butterflies, dragonflies, tarantulas, desert pupfish

DIRECTIONS: From Phoenix, go east on U.S. Route 60 to Milepost 223, then turn right (south) into the park entrance.

ENTRY FEE: Yes

TRAILS: 1.5-mile primary loop plus another 1.5 miles of trails, easy to moderate

SERVICES AND FACILITIES: Arboretum, visitors center, exhibits, restrooms, guided hikes, presentations, classes, food, picnic area, gift shop

MORE INFORMATION: 520-689-2811 or www. azstateparks.com/Parks/BOTH

SOUTHWESTERN ARIZONA
IMPERIAL NATIONAL WILDLIFE REFUGE
Yuma

Arizona is home to eight national wildlife refuges, but Imperial is unique, offering a dramatic mix of desert badlands and river oases. In the calm, blue backwaters of the Colorado River, native and migratory water birds forage. But away from the marshes, the terrain is exquisitely windswept, with minerals painting the sand in hues of red, pink and yellow, and rangy desert plants, tangled ironwood trees and scented creosote, speckling the panorama. Within this

HOW TO USE BINOCULARS

Before looking for animals, make sure your binoculars are properly set. Shift the barrels to the proper width for your eyes; then, pick an object, close your right eye and roll the focus wheel until the image is clear. Close your left eye and fine-tune the diopter setting — usually on the right eyepiece — to sharpen the image. Then, open both eyes; if the image is not clear, repeat the steps. When viewing wildlife, always use your naked eye to find the animal. Visually lock on, then raise the binoculars to your eyes and adjust only the focus wheel as needed. Here's a fun tip: Looking backward and up close through the lenses will give you a macro view of tiny things.

spartan scenery, more animals flourish than first meet the eye. Located in the hottest, driest region of the state — less than 4 inches of annual rainfall — residents have adapted to survive. Many scurry into crevices and live nocturnal lives. Those that venture into daylight are masked by camouflage, requiring careful, active surveillance to be seen. Search for lizards in the rocky areas, hares and quail in the underbrush, and colorful songbirds among the densest leaves. Be early to rise, and an extra-special sighting, like a bighorn drinking from the river, may await. Nearby Kofa National Wildlife Refuge (north on U.S. Route 95) is also worth visiting; its jagged pinnacles afford habitat for a considerable population of bighorns.

ESTABLISHED: 1941

SIZE: 25,768 acres, including 30 miles of lower Colorado River

ELEVATION: 180 to 1,085 feet

HABITAT: Desert scrub, riparian areas, wetlands (marshes and backwaters)

WILDLIFE INCLUDES: Mule deer, bighorn sheep, bobcats, jackrabbits, pallid bats, turkey vultures, burrowing owls, roadrunners, Gila woodpeckers, Gambel's quail, phainopeplas, Western tanagers, hummingbirds, black and Say's phoebes, ash-throated flycatchers, cliff swallows, verdins, house finches, herons, Western grebes, American coots, killdeer, buffleheads, desert tortoises, desert spiny and whiptail lizards, common kingsnakes, diamondback rattlesnakes, desert pupfish, approximately 200 species of migratory birds (winter)

DIRECTIONS: From Yuma, go north on U.S. Route 95 to Martinez Lake Road, located between mileposts 46 and 47. Turn left onto Martinez Lake Road and continue to Red Cloud Mine Road, a maintained dirt road. Follow the brown signs for 3 miles to the refuge.

ENTRY FEE: No

TRAILS: Painted Desert (1.3 miles, moderate) and Meers Point (0.8 miles, easy), plus off-trail hiking allowed in the 15,000-acre wilderness area

SERVICES AND FACILITIES: Visitors center, exhibits, restrooms, observation tower, lookout points, interpretive signs, boat ramp (limited use)

MORE INFORMATION: 928-783-3371 or www.fws.gov/refuge/imperial

SOUTHEASTERN ARIZONA

CHIRICAHUA NATIONAL MONUMENT
Willcox

After a pilgrimage across flaxen grasslands, wending up the tree-lined road into Chiricahua National Monument is like arriving at one of nature's finest castles. Columned stone formations called hoodoos rise from the earth like gentle goliaths welcoming visitors to their extraordinary kingdom. The Chiricahua range, the largest "sky island" in the Madrean Archipelago (see page 11), is world-renowned for its biological diversity and offers the broadest wildlife viewing opportunities of Arizona's 14 national monuments. At its interior, mountain peaks stretch to the horizon, their slopes stippled with elegant pines and shaggy oaks, twisted red manzanitas and the spires of succulent yuccas. Seventy species of mammals, including rare Coues deer and Chiricahua fox squirrels, plus myriad birds, reptiles, amphibians and invertebrates, inhabit this flamboyant landscape. Be sure to follow the Echo Canyon Loop trail down to the creek, with passage

Chiricahua National Monument

through natural stone tunnels carved by ancient wind and water. The surrounding national forest can also be explored. And while in the region, consider a trip to Whitewater Draw Wildlife Area (south on State Route 181 and U.S. Route 191, off Central Highway below Elfrida), which attracts abundant fauna to its wetlands.

ESTABLISHED: 1924

SIZE: 11,985 acres

ELEVATION: 5,124 to 7,310 feet

HABITAT: Forests, woodlands, grasslands, riparian areas

WILDLIFE INCLUDES: Coues deer, mule deer, black bears, cougars, ringtails, coatis, jackrabbits, spotted skunks, lesser long-nosed bats, gray foxes, badgers, porcupines, Botta's pocket gophers, Chiricahua fox squirrels, ground squirrels, cliff chipmunks, Ord's kangaroo rats, packrats, bald and golden eagles, owls, hawks, wild turkeys, Montezuma quail, acorn woodpeckers, Western tanagers, brown-headed cowbirds, house finches, Sonoran mountain kingsnakes, coralsnakes, Chiricahua leopard frogs, canyon treefrogs, millipedes, centipedes, butterflies

DIRECTIONS: From Willcox, go south on State Route 186 for 32 miles to State Route 181. Turn left (east) onto SR 181 and continue 4 miles to the entrance station.

ENTRY FEE: No

TRAILS: 17 miles of day-use trails, from easy (0.2 to 1.2 miles) to moderate (1.8 to 4.8 miles) to strenuous (5.4 to 9.5 miles), plus an 8-mile, paved scenic drive

SERVICES AND FACILITIES: Visitors centers, exhibits, restrooms, presentations, guided hikes, interpretive signs, campground, gift shop

MORE INFORMATION: 520-824-3560 or www.nps.gov/chir

Mountain lion (female), southeast of Flagstaff

When You Go...

Hike the trail less traveled. Wildlife typically avoids concentrated human traffic. By selecting paths farther from the hub, you increase your odds of glimpsing those more secretive species.

See the sun rise (or set). Most mammals are crepuscular or nocturnal, so midday sightings are typically sparse. Be out by first light or after nightfall (use caution and a headlamp in the dark).

Dress wisely. Bright, noisy clothes will send wildlife into hiding. Choose neutral colors in soft fabrics that won't rustle when you walk.

Search near water. Animals from surrounding habitats approach water sources to drink, so take time to quietly explore lakeshores, riverbanks, brooks and ponds.

Take binoculars. They will zoom you up close to the animals you spy, taking away any pressure to pursue, which could unduly disrupt their natural activities.

Look up. There often are birds gracing the skies or watching the world (including you) from an elevated perch. There's a chart for identifying large birds in flight on page 68.

Look down and around. You might spot signs of animals that passed through: scat, tracks (see opposite page) or lost feathers. Or you might discover someone's home: nest, hole or web.

Really **look.** Stay alert to movement and focus "through" vegetation for animal shapes. Paying sharp attention without becoming absorbed in thoughts or scenery takes practice.

Use your guidebook. Identify a species by shape, size, color and range. Knowing which one you are viewing and something about its natural history will make the sighting more meaningful.

Sit and watch. If you are silent and still, wildlife that disappeared on your arrival may re-emerge and give you a special chance to observe some natural behavior.

Listen. The sounds of nature are marvelous — the chirp of a bird, buzz of a bee or yip of a coyote lends to our fullest outdoor experience. Savor the earthly aromas, too.

Keep your distance. Never chase, touch or feed wildlife, as it has unintended negative impacts on the animals, including stress, desensitization and even disease.

Leave no trace. Be respectful by staying on the trail, talking softly, packing out your trash and leaving nature's precious belongings where you found them.

CHRISTINA BOGGS

Tracks

mountain lion, bobcat

bear

wolf, coyote, fox

raccoon

squirrel

rat, mouse

rabbit, hare

lizard

porcupine

skunk

opossum

otter

elk, deer

bird

javelina

toad, frog

(webbed)

(zygodactyl)

(perching)

Arizona Wildlife Organizations

Have you found a sick, injured or orphaned wild animal? The following contacts are trained and licensed to provide rescue and/or rehabilitation for native Arizona species, and some, marked with an asterisk (*), may even be able to assist statewide. Depending on your location and concern, you may be referred to other organizations or individual rehabilitators not listed here. By the way, if you want to support (or work with) wildlife, these nonprofits run on donations and volunteers — they are a meaningful place to contribute.

Adobe Mountain Wildlife Center (birds, mammals, reptiles) in Phoenix, 623-582-9806 or www.azwildlifecenter.net
*ized**Arizona Game and Fish Department** (birds, mammals, reptiles) 602-942-3000
Bradshaw Mountain Wildlife Association (mammals) in Mayer, 928-632-9559 or www.bradshawmountainwildlife.com
East Valley Wildlife (birds) in Chandler, 480-814-9339 or www.eastvalleywildlife.org
*__**Liberty Wildlife** (birds, mammals, reptiles) in Scottsdale/Phoenix, 480-998-5550 or www.libertywildlife.org
Phoenix Herpetological Society (reptiles) in Scottsdale, 480-513-4377 or www.phoenixherp.com
*__**Southwest Wildlife** (birds, mammals, reptiles) in Scottsdale/Rio Verde, 480-471-9109 or www.southwestwildlife.org
Tucson Wildlife Center (birds, mammals) in Tucson, 520-290-9453 or www.tucsonwildlife.com
Wild at Heart (raptors) in Cave Creek/Phoenix, 480-595-5047 or www.wildatheartraptors.org

Glossary

KEY: noun (*n.*), verb (*v.*), adjective (*adj.*), plural (*pl.*), example e.g.

adaptation evolutionary trait (physical or behavioral) that increases odds of survival
amphibian ectothermic vertebrate of class *Amphibia*; aquatic larvae usually develop into lunged adults
anatid water bird of order *Anatidae*; duck, swan or goose
Anthropocene geological epoch (since 1800s) in which humans have significant impact on global ecosystems
antlers bony growths on the heads of certain animals (e.g. elk, deer); typically shed yearly
anuran amphibian of order *Anura*; frog (also see bufonid)
apex predator carnivore at the top of the food chain, with no natural predators
aposematic coloration that warns potential predators of venom, poison or distasteful toxins
aquatic relating to or living in water
arboreal relating to or living in trees
arid dry; describes a barren landscape receiving little to no rain
avian bird; relating to birds
bajada fanned slope of sand, silt, gravel or clay from mountain base, created by water flow
bill toothless mandibles of a bird, sometimes called a beak

biodiversity the variety of all life in a particular region or habitat

biology study of living organisms; biological (*adj.*)

bird endothermic vertebrate of class *Aves*; egg-laying, possessing feathers and wings, most can fly

bird of prey raptor; carnivorous bird, usually possessing talons; e.g. eagle, hawk, falcon, owl

breeding season period of time during which a species engages in reproductive behavior (courtship, mating)

brood litter; family of young offspring hatched, born or raised at the same time; to brood (*v.*)

brumation hibernation-like dormancy (extended torpor) of a reptile during winter

bufonid anuran of family *Bufonidae*; toad

camouflage appearance or coloring that blends into the environment, making detection difficult

canid (also canine) carnivore of family *Canidae*; dog

cannibalism eating one's own kind; cannibalistic (*adj.*)

canyon deep, narrow valley with steep cliff walls, often with stream or river at bottom

carapace top shell of certain animals (e.g. turtle)

carnivorous eats other animals; carnivore (*n.*)

carrion remains of dead animal(s), often fed on by other animals

chiropteran flying mammal of order *Chiroptera*; bat

chytridiomycosis infectious fungal disease caused by an aquatic pathogen, globally killing off frog populations

cienega wet meadow, often created by an underground spring

clade modern taxonomic group based on genetic ancestry through molecular sequencing

class taxonomic level that divides into orders

cloaca single opening for intestinal, urinary and genital tracts in certain animals; also called a vent

clutch all eggs deposited during one laying

colonial living or nesting collectively in clustered groups

conservation protective management of natural resources to preserve and restore ecosystems and wildlife

courtship social interactions between male and female that lead to mating

crepuscular active at dusk and dawn

crop expandable pouch found in the throat of certain birds, used to store food for digestion

cryptic coloring ability of certain animals to change color for camouflage

desert scrub arid habitat with sparse vegetation; 80 to 7,200 feet elevation; 8 to 17 inches annual rainfall

detritus particles of decomposing organic matter

dewlap loose skin on lower neck of certain animals, which may or may not be controlled

diurnal active during the day

dorsal upper side; back area

dune mound of windblown sand

echolocation ability to emit/receive/decipher sound waves to interpret surroundings; to echolocate (*v.*)

ecosystem complex network of interacting life forms and their environment

ectothermic unable to regulate body temperature, reliant upon surroundings for heating and cooling

endangered species at serious risk of extinction or extirpation; protected under Endangered Species Act

Endangered Species Act established by Congress in 1973 to list and protect endangered and threatened species

endemic native and limited to a particular area

endothermic able to regulate body temperature, self-heating/cooling

excrement animal waste; also called feces, scat, dung, guano (bats and seabirds)

extinction point at which no more living animals of a particular species exist on the planet

extirpation when a species no longer exists in a particular part of its original range; a local extinction

family taxonomic level below order, which divides into genera

fauna animal life; all animals in a particular region or habitat

felid (also feline) carnivore of family *Felidae*; cat

fertilization fusion of egg and sperm to begin life; to fertilize (*v.*)

fish (bony) ectothermic vertebrate of class *Osteichthyes*; egg-laying, fully aquatic with fins and gills

fledgling young bird that has left the nest, usually with primary feathers to start flying; to fledge (*v.*)

flight feathers large, rigid feathers on bird wings and tail that aid in flight; also called primaries

flora plant life; all plants in a particular region or habitat

forage to search for food

forest high-elevation habitat with pine, fir and/or spruce trees; 6,500 to 11,500 feet elevation; 18 to 39 inches annual rainfall

fry hatchling fish

genetic relating to the transmission of genes (DNA) from an animal to its descendants

genus taxonomic level below family, which divides into species; genera (*pl.*)

gestation period of development inside the mother, before birth

gills respiratory organs that extract oxygen from water, found in fish and young amphibians

gorget iridescent throat patch on male hummingbird, flashes vibrantly in sunlight

grassland grassy habitat, mostly open, flat or rolling terrain; 3,600 to 11,480 feet elevation; 10 to 20 inches annual rainfall

hemotoxin chemical in venom that causes extensive bleeding and tissue damage

herbivorous eats plant matter; herbivore (*n.*)

herpetologist biologist who studies reptiles and/or amphibians

hibernation extended period of winter dormancy with reduced metabolism and body temperature

horns hard, permanent growths of bone and keratin on the head of certain animals (e.g. sheep)

hybrid the resulting offspring from interbreeding of two separate species

incubation period of development inside the egg, before hatching

invertebrate animal without a spine; includes insects, arachnids, worms and crustaceans

juvenile young animal; not yet sexually mature or of adult size

keel ridge-like in structure; the breastbone of a bird; "keeled" scales on certain reptiles

keystone species animal that plays a imperative role in the functioning of an ecosystem

larva juvenile form of certain animal species; for insects it is usually worm-like; larvae (*pl.*)

life cycle stages of animal life, including birth/hatching, growth/metamorphosis, reproduction, death

mammal endothermic vertebrate of class *Mammalia*; grows hair, gives live birth, offspring suckle milk

marsupial mammal that carries and nurses developing offspring in an abdominal pouch

metachromatism change in color due to environmental factors, especially temperature

metamorphosis physical transformation of amphibians and insects to their adult form; to metamorphose (*v.*)

migration seasonal movement of certain animals from between locations; to migrate (*v.*), migratory (*adj.*)

mimicry imitating an unrelated species for some benefit (usually protection); mimic (*n.*), to mimic (*v.*)

mobbing anti-predator behavior, mostly in birds; harassing, dive-bombing, defecating on intruders

molt to shed a body covering of skin (e.g. snakes), feathers, fur or exoskeleton

monogamous describes a bonded and exclusive mating pair

monsoon season Southwestern period of storms, generally July through September; provides up to 70 percent of annual rainfall

montane of or relating to mountainous habitat

natal relating to birth, in either place or time

native naturally occurring; having always lived in a designated area

neurotoxin chemical in venom that damages the central nervous system

nocturnal active at night

offspring genetic descendant(s) of an animal

omnivorous eats both plant matter and other animals; omnivore (*n.*)

order taxonomic level below class, which divides into families

ornithologist biologist who studies birds

ovoviviparous form of reproduction; embryotic eggs are retained in mother's body, followed by live birth

parotoid gland near eye of certain amphibians (especially toads), secretes milky toxin to deter predators

passerine "song" bird of order *Passeriformes*, more than half of all avian species; toes arranged for perching

plankton tiny organisms that drift in aquatic habitats

plumage feathering on a bird; plume (singular, one feather)

pollinator animal that moves pollen between flowers, aiding fertilization of the plant

precocial describes an animal that is able to move and feed at birth or hatching

predatory defines an animal that captures and eats other animals; predator (*n.*)

prehensile able to grasp; describes certain animals' tails (e.g. opossum, monkey)

prey animal hunted and eaten by a predator

reptile ectothermic vertebrate of class *Reptilia*; egg-laying, possessing scaled skin

reticulated net-like pattern having interlacing lines

riparian habitat found along rivers, streams, creeks and other waterways

rodent mammal of order *Rodentia*, paired incisor teeth continuously grow; e.g. beaver, squirrel, rat

roost location where birds or bats sleep, often in groups; to roost (*v.*)

rut breeding season of certain hoofed mammals; males may compete for mating rights

sexual dimorphism physical differences between male and female of the same species

sky island isolated mountain with endemic species that do not inhabit or cross the surrounding lowland

spawning method of aquatic reproduction; eggs and sperm simultaneously released into the water

species taxonomic level below genus, which may or may not divide into subspecies

subspecies lowest taxonomic level, below species

subterranean relating to or living underground

tadpole aquatic larva of frogs and toads, possessing gills and tail

talons long, sharp, grasping claws of a raptor

talus rock fragments broken from canyon walls or mountain slopes

taxonomy science of classifying biological groups based on shared characteristics; taxonomic (*adj.*)

terrestrial relating to or living on the ground

territorial being defensive of one's home range; willing to compete to dominate a particular area

threatened species likely to become endangered; protected under Endangered Species Act

torpor short period of inactivity associated with reduced metabolism and body temperature

ungulate hoofed (usually herbivorous) mammal

venom fluid produced by certain animals to be injected into prey or used for defense

ventral underside; belly area

vertebrate animal of subphylum *Vertebrata*, having a spine; mammal, bird, reptile, amphibian, fish

viper venomous serpent of family *Viperidae*; rattlesnake

webbed foot toes connected from base to tip with thin skin to aid in paddling water

wetlands terrain that is wet or watery; e.g. cienegas, marshes, pools

whitewash white stains on natural objects from an accumulation of bird excrement (buildup of urates)

wingspan measurement from wingtip to wingtip when wings fully extended

woodland habitat marked by oak, piñon and/or juniper trees; 4,250 to 7,500 feet elevation; 6 to 24 inches annual rainfall

zygodactyl X-shaped foot; having two toes pointing forward and two back; e.g. roadrunner, woodpecker

World of Wonder

Arizona has long been a mecca for birders, with about 500 bird species documented within our borders. Many subtropical species, including five-striped sparrows, elegant trogons and buff-collared nightjars, frequent Southern Arizona during the warm months. Hummingbirds are abundant, and the attentive birder may encounter up to 15 species in a single canyon in the Huachuca Mountains. During the winter, a multitude of raptors, waterfowl and songbirds can be seen in urban centers, on agricultural lands and at natural areas throughout the state. The Arizona Game and Fish Department's Whitewater Draw Wildlife Area is the wintering roost and loafing site for thousands of sandhill cranes, in addition to many other species of fowl. But what even many enthusiasts don't realize is that Arizona is much more than just birds.

Arizona ranks third in the nation (behind California and Texas) for biodiversity, which makes it a top destination for wildlife viewers of all kinds. Enthusiasts come from around the world to enjoy our state's diverse fauna. Of the 800 species of wildlife managed by Game and Fish (not including insects, arachnids and other arthropods), roughly 138 are native mammals, ranging from endangered species such as jaguars and black-footed ferrets to bison and shrews. Most of these are seldom seen by the casual viewer, but all play a role in the health and stability of our state's ecological systems. In contrast, pronghorns, deer, elk and a variety of smaller mammals are common sights in places they inhabit. But even these can be difficult to see if you don't know when and where to look.

To help people find and connect with wildlife, Game and Fish has started a wildlife-viewing program called World of Wonder. It hosts wildlife webcams that can be viewed from the comfort of home, along with field-based tours, staged throughout the state, that focus on local wildlife and are led by knowledgeable biologists. Many World of Wonder outings are free, while others require a nominal fee to cover expenses.

Finding and learning about wildlife is easier with seasoned experts who share their field experience and insights with participants. Look for these programs on the Game and Fish website, www.azgfd.gov, or contact Game and Fish and ask about wildlife viewing programs in your area.

— Randall D. Babb, manager of the Watchable Wildlife Program
of the Arizona Game and Fish Department

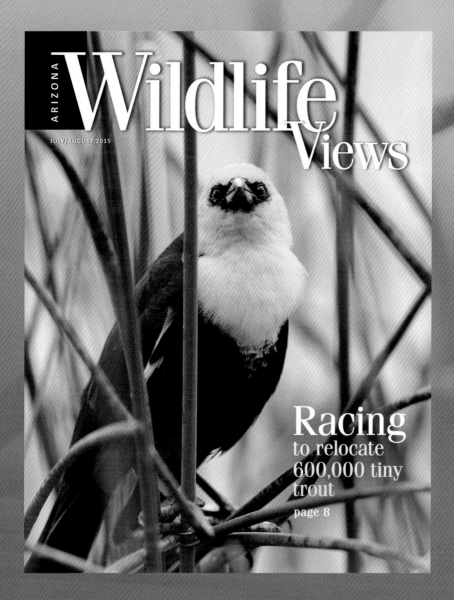

Index